A *word about thi* Toastmasters In

Who needs another book on public speaking, let alone a series of them? After all, this is a skill best learned by practice and "just doing it," you say.

But if practice is the best solution to public speaking excellence, why is this world so full of speakers who can't speak effectively? Consider politicians, business executives, sales professionals, teachers, trainers, clerics, and even "professional" speakers who often fail to reach their audiences because they make elementary mistakes, such as speaking too fast or too long, failing to prepare adequately, and forgetting to consider their audiences.

As we experience in Toastmasters Clubs, practice and feedback are important and play major roles in developing your speaking skills. But insight and tips from people who have already been where you are might help ease some bumps along the road, reinforce some basic public speaking techniques, and provide guidance on handling special speech problems and situations you may encounter. The purpose of *The Essence of Public Speaking Series* is to help you prepare for the unexpected, warn you of the pitfalls, and help you ensure that the message you want to give is indeed the same one the audience hears.

This series features the accumulated wisdom of experts in various speech-related fields. The books are written by trained professionals who have spent decades writing and delivering speeches and training others. The series covers the spectrum of speaking, including writing, using humor, customizing particular topics for various audiences, and incorporating technology into presentations.

Whether you are an inexperienced or seasoned public speaker, *The Essence of Public Speaking Series* belongs on your bookshelf because no matter how good you are, there is always room for improvement. The books are your key to becoming a more effective speaker. Do you have the self-discipline to put into practice the techniques and advice offered in them?

I honestly believe that every person who truly wants to become a confident and eloquent public speaker can become one. Success or failure depends on attitude. There is no such thing as a "hopeless case." If you want to enhance your personal and professional progress, I urge you to become a better public speaker by doing two things:

- Read these books.
- Get on your feet and practice what you've learned.

Terrence J. McCann
Executive Director, Toastmasters International

Choosing Powerful Words

CHOOSING POWERFUL WORDS

Eloquence That Works

RONALD H. CARPENTER
University of Florida

WILLIAM D. THOMPSON
Series Editor

ALLYN AND BACON

Boston London Toronto Sydney Tokyo Singapore

Contents

Preface

You can! You, too, can be that stylist and a slogan-maker whose sentences may become "sound bites" on the evening news or quoted in newspaper accounts the day after you utter them in a speech. You, too, can write sentences that are endowed with the eloquence that makes them potentially as memorable and quotable as those most familiar and persuasive statements made by speakers such as Abraham Lincoln, Franklin Roosevelt, and John Kennedy. And you can do so easily by applying the precepts and techniques described in this book.

My claims may seem presumptuous. After all, a host of factors (some of which I describe briefly in Chapter 1) seemingly preclude their possibility. For several reasons outlined below, however, I make my claim without reservation, categorically, firmly.

Like many other worthy books about effective communication, this one is founded on a wide range of evidence about those factors that endow a speaker's words with the power to influence other people. Some of this evidence comes from rhetorical theorists of the past, whose observations about persuasive language remain relevant. Their pragmatic and perceptive observations are complemented in this book by contemporary research conducted by psycholinguists, psychologists, rhetorical critics, and communication and persuasion theorists. Moreover, my career of published research about style in discourse—in scholarly books, book chapters, and numerous academic journal articles—has confirmed, clarified, and refined many of these principles about language effectiveness, and these findings inform this book as well. You will find abundant references to my research.

More important, the teachability of the principles I advance in this book has been honed over the years in my popular speechwriting course here at the University of Florida, in which students learn to write their sentences in the same memorable and persuasive conformations that characterized the speaking of Lincoln, Roosevelt, and Kennedy, for examples. In this course, college students make significant progress toward a prowess with language that lasts for the rest of their lives as business and professional people. As one of my students later wrote, "I use what I learned in everything I write, whether it be a simple letter or complex brief. I know the importance of writing well. . . . Today, I have a reputation as a skilled writer and I feel I owe a great deal of that reputation to your training."

Most important, however, the precepts and principles taught in this book are highly relevant for business and professional people who no longer have easy access to academic courses to improve their communication effectiveness—but nevertheless recognize the importance of this skill and want to achieve greater proficiency efficiently. Many of the practice exercises in this book are ones that I use as a consultant with my training sessions for a wide range of business, professional, and military groups. In my workshop-seminar, "Write Well—Right Now," participants in only one morning or afternoon session make significant improvements in their abilities to phrase their utterances in more advantageous ways than before. For nearly two decades, this training session has been repeated several times at each State Meeting of the California Bar Association. The program also is offered to incoming classes of officers each year at the U.S. Naval War College in Newport, Rhode Island. A U.S. Navy admiral attests that for a major address he recently gave, the training "allowed me to give the speech with total confidence in its phrasing." Similar acclaim for the "Write Well—Right Now" seminar has come from other groups as diverse as hospital administrators, corporate executives, and civic leaders. The speechwriters and

Public Relations Advisory Council of the U.S. Postmaster General found the program "practical and inspiring."

As you can see, what I teach in this book is informed by relevant research and careful scholarship about how to pick the best words and arrange them in their best orders. The precepts used to achieve greater power with words are eminently teachable, having been carefully honed in the classroom. And a host of professional people testify that greater prowess with words can be attained efficiently by mastering the precepts explained in this book. So come for some hours of instruction about persuasive style in discourse—and go with years of confidence in your capabilities as a communicator.

Ronald H. Carpenter
University of Florida

1 ORALITY, RHETORIC, AND ELOQUENCE

Sight isolates, sound incorporates.

Father Walter J. Ong, *Orality and Literacy*

Words work. With language in sentences and longer statements, people may exert magnificent influence over others. From their first experiences with differentiated speech sounds, children learn that important lesson: starting by calling "ma ma," progressing to "I'm hungry," and subsequently to "May I use the car tonight; I'll be careful and be home early—and I promise to mow the lawn the first thing tomorrow morning." Then, as people acquire further communication prowess, they appreciate even more how their words in sentences can cause other people to be entertained or interested, better informed, or persuaded to attitudes and actions. And the best words in their best orders work even more effectively to influence others through communication—particularly public speaking.

Over the centuries, relevant rhetorical theory has identified and explained principles and techniques by which eloquence comes to characterize those words that attain power in public speaking. Contemporary evidence about that effectiveness also comes from psychologists, psycholinguists, and communication and persuasion theorists, as well as scholars in still other fields. Together, these findings complement one another to offer guidelines about ways in which public speakers—indeed, communicators in any verbal mode—can enhance the impress of their words. We all are familiar with speeches and even single sentences that strongly influenced the attitudes and actions of others. And if sentences from political figures seemingly are prominent among these examples, the reason is that these individuals' words often are among the more widely known for persuasiveness. These salient instances of effectiveness in the past may constitute the most meaningful exemplars for speakers in the present—whether on the political hustings, in corporate boardrooms, or in myriad situations in between. The potential power of words in public speaking is understood more fully, however, by appreciating at the outset the inherently pervasive and persuasive essence of orality.

ORALITY

On any given day in contemporary society, people we would influence with our spoken words likely have been exposed very recently to thousands of other words, whether heard face-to-face from other people or over the telephone or read in various sources. We all look at newspapers, billboards, correspondence, and—increasingly—computer screens. By the 1970s, the United States had approximately 1,750 daily newspapers printing nearly 63 million copies per day. Nearly 6,500 radio stations could be heard through 300 million radio sets (or three for every two people). In over 98 percent of all American homes, at least one television set was turned on for an average of five hours per day. An average American watched TV for two and one-half hours each day. Today, easy access to words spoken or written by other people is even more widespread. An average American family now likely has two television sets and five or six radios, counting clock radios, car radios, and omnipresent transistor radios that accompany people in a wide range of their activities. Add the amount of conversation that audience members have engaged in previous to their hearing a speech—or immediately thereafter. Then add personal computers, an increasingly significant source of messages that compound the problem. Computer screens in schools, homes, and workplaces across the country add immeasurably to the vast numbers of words to which we could respond every day. With so many media disseminating messages, Americans today surely are less the communicators, however, and more the recipients of communication.[1]

Thousands upon thousands of words per day try to interest us, teach us, and persuade us to attitudes and actions. If spoken statements—or written ones, for that matter—are to compete successfully among those myriad messages, they require advantages accrued from those subtle adjustments in word choices and word arrangements that the most effective communicators have used to enhance the power of their sentences. After all, public speaking is a highly fallible mode of communication. In some cases, audiences *listen cognitively* to only 50 percent of the words they *hear physiologically*; and in other cases, up to 90 percent of what people "learn" as a result of listening to a speech has nothing to do with the manifest content of that discourse but consists rather of the "information" communicated by a speaker's mode of dress, physical mannerisms, or other elements extraneous to the message itself. Therefore, this moral is inescapable: to compete successfully amid the myriad messages to which their listeners recently have been exposed, public speakers *must* be skilled. For face-to-face oral communication potentially *is* an inexorably pervasive mode of imparting information and exerting influence.

Consider how people learned about the assassination of John F. Kennedy. The president was shot at 12:30 P.M. (CST) on November 22, 1963, and doctors announced his death 30 minutes later. By that time, over two thirds of those Americans old enough to understand who the president was already knew of the assassination. After another hour had passed, nine tenths of those Americans knew that Kennedy had died; and four hours later—five and one-half hours after the event—virtually everyone in the United States—99.8 percent of those people— knew that the president had been assassinated. In a controlled study to identify how people had acquired that knowledge, investigators ascertained that "less than half of these people got their initial information from the mass media; most people first heard about the event from other people." Yes, Americans now live in a vast "communication mosaic" of competing messages.[2] But when important ideas must be communicated, whether to inform or persuade, people likely acquire those meanings from someone talking directly to them. Moreover, formal public speaking per se often is the vehicle by which attitudes and actions of listeners are influenced—because of that significant factor known as "orality."

When describing "the primacy of oral speech," Walter J. Ong, a Jesuit priest who has written about language with great insight, notes that of all the languages—perhaps thousands in the course of human history—most have never been written at all. Yes, in some societies, writing and literacy became increasingly important, such as during the English Renaissance; but despite the vast amount of what is read in contemporary society, written texts do not diminish the power potentially derived from orality. After all, reading a text entails converting it to sound, "aloud or in the imagination, syllable–by–syllable." And for communicators who would influence other people, another advantage accrues from the "psychodynamics of orality" that bestow "great power" upon what is articulated aloud in discourse.

> Sound exists only when it is going out of existence. . . .
> When I pronounce the word "permanence," by the time
> I get to the "–nence," the " perma–" is gone. . . . If I
> stop the movement of sound, I have nothing—only
> silence, no sound at all. . . . Vision can register motion,
> but . . . we often reduce motion to a series of still shots
> the better to see what motion is. There is no equivalent
> of a still shot for sound. An oscillogram is silent.

Thus, sound—particularly as it functions in oral discourse—is
"dynamic."[3]

In an age attuned to visual impressions from television,
culture admittedly is replete with "still shots" lingering in our
consciousness: President Kennedy at the moment of being
assassinated during a motorcade in Dallas, Texas; his young
son, still a toddler, saluting as his father's casket passes by on a
horse–drawn caisson; and the president's assassin, Lee Harvey
Oswald, at the instant of being shot, in turn, by Jack Ruby.
Even before television, some photographs accomplished as
persuasion what thousands of spoken and written words could
not. For Americans at the advent of World War II, the picture
of a Chinese baby crying amid the rubble after a Japanese air
raid was instrumental in crystallizing sentiment against Japan.
Before that widely published photograph, the Japanese were
deemed rather innocuous; after it, they were perceived increasingly as barbaric. But despite the visual impress of television—
and increasingly omnipresent computer screens—orality
remains a significant mode for persuasion.

An apt epigram from Father Ong synthesizes the potential
power of oral discourse: "sight isolates, sound incorporates."

> Whereas sight situates the observer outside what he
> views, at a distance, sound pours into the hearer. . . .
> Vision comes into a human being from one direction at
> a time: to look at a room or a landscape, I must move
> my eyes around from one part to another. When I hear,

> however, I gather sound simultaneously from every
> direction at once. . . . You can immerse yourself in hear-
> ing, in sound. There is no way to immerse yourself simi-
> larly in sight.[4]

This distinction between "isolates" and "incorporates" has
profound implications for public speakers. Whereas vision is a
"dissecting" sense, sound is a "unifying" one. The goal of seeing is "clarity and distinctness, a taking apart"; conversely, listening is a "putting together" with "unifying" and "harmo-
nizing" tendencies. Furthermore, although the primacy of
orality in earlier cultures yielded to print in the English
Renaissance, electronic media now foster a "new orality" with
"striking resemblances" to the old in its capability to create a
"communal sense." Listening to spoken words can turn hearers into "a group, a true audience," whereas reading turns
individuals "in on themselves." Because electronic media
reach such vast numbers of listeners, orality generates groups
"immeasurably larger" than those that existed earlier in cultures that were primarily oral.[5] Opportunities for speakers to
achieve impact thus are multiplied exponentially.

The "group" aspect of orality has important implications
for speakers and their audiences—whether assembled in audi-
toriums, churches, legislatures, convention meeting rooms,
briefings, courts of law, or corporate board rooms. In any of
these places, listeners are aware of one another, and yet all
respond to the same stimulus of the speaker because of the
"psychodynamics of orality."

> When a speaker is addressing an audience, the members
> of the audience normally become a unity. . . . If the
> speaker asks the audience to read a handout provided
> for them, as each reader enters into his or her own pri-
> vate reading world, the unity of the audience is shat-
> tered, to be reestablished only when oral speech begins
> again.[6]

If writing and print "isolate," speakers before groups in all likelihood are all the more persuasive *because* listeners are responding in *face-to-face* situations.

RHETORIC

Rhetoric is not a pejorative word! And the power of words that is inherent in "orality" is complemented by an accurate assessment of what it means to be rhetorical. In a widespread—but unfortunate—usage, the word *rhetoric* too often is preceded by the adjective *empty* to characterize what "other" people say as manipulative or groundless emotional appeals, in stark contrast to discourse that only "tells it like it is." Accurately, rhetoric is "the rationale of informative and suasory discourse" whose "central" function is *"adjusting ideas to people and people to ideas."*[7] For 24 centuries, the best minds in Western Civilization sought to identify and explain those factors in discourse that enable speakers to be effective. That composite lore is rhetorical theory, and sophisticated scholarship in recent years has refined and corroborated many of those traditional factors that enable speakers to be effective in public discourse.

The most persuasive discourse is derived from finding and selecting those elements of content and form that most likely will achieve intended impress upon audiences. Any effective speaker, therefore, must be what Rod Hart and Don Burks characterize as that *"rhetorically sensitive person . . . willing to undergo the strain of adaptation"* in order "to deal better with the very different perceptual world of the Other." Although someone might "tell it like it is" from a "determination of which ideas are to be made known," that particular "it" does not necessarily prescribe the specific *"rhetorical configurations which can make 'it' social fare."* The most effective speakers have a "communicative humility, a realization that the idea as first constituted in my head may not be worth a damn when it confronts an unknown quantity—the Other." So those speakers will "process" and then choose among all possible verbal strategies *before* giving utterance to an idea."[8] After all, oral discourse is predicated upon an inescapable fact: the meanings evoked in listeners by spoken words are not necessarily the ones intended by speakers. In a landmark statement, Andrew Weaver and Ordean Ness isolated the nature of oral discourse when they suggested that a speaker *"stirs up* meanings (ideas and feelings)" in an audience by "inducing" those people "to recall . . . past experiences. . . . As speakers, the best that we can do is to use audible and/or visible symbols which may touch off in our listeners certain elements of their past experiences; this we try to do in such a manner that the listeners will produce for themselves the meaningful patterns which we want them to have."[9]

The word choices and their syntactical arrangements that likely attain the greatest power evolve when speakers base their statements upon accurate assessments of the "rhetorical situation" in which they will function. A speaking situation is "rhetorical" when three factors are present: (1) an exigency or imperfection that can be modified by discourse, (2) an audience capable of implementing the change advocated by communication, and (3) constraints operative upon a communicator to produce discourse that is a fitting response to that exigency and for that audience.[10] The changes recommended and perhaps brought about by discourse are as varied as the widely differing audiences found in churches, political meetings, courtrooms, banquet halls, legislatures, corporate boardrooms, classrooms, or any gatherings wherein people assemble. Moreover, "fitting" responses by speakers are equally varied according to exigencies being confronted as well as places in which speeches are delivered. But *one* constraint upon speakers is sufficiently universal to be significant in *any* rhetorical situation: the absolute imperative for speakers to make their specific sentences salient among all the communication in that vast "mosaic" of words that confront Americans daily.

America changed. As people in the twentieth century increasingly left their farms and small towns to reside in large cities or urban sprawls, they concomitantly lost a hallmark of earlier American life—direct participation in the discourse of practical affairs, whether in New England town meetings or Grange halls in rural areas. In urbanized society, after fighting rush hour traffic while returning home from work, few people go out again to meetings or larger groups in which they articulate their views on current issues. Rather, they seem content to sit before television sets and listen to others' views, particularly those of articulate people.

Americans are reticent partly because of a "literacy crisis" created when Soviet scientists were the first to place a satellite in orbit around the earth. Sputnik was a small object with a giant influence upon American education. Based on fear that the Soviet Union had surpassed the United States in technology, public education was restructured to catch up; sciences and mathematics were emphasized in the public schools; but because the school day is only so long, when some subjects were emphasized, others were deemphasized. Language arts, for speaking and writing, often suffered. Moreover, that part of the curriculum was hampered when teachers had five language arts classes per day, each with 30 or more students (who preferred watching television to reading books). Teachers who graded 150 compositions with each writing assignment did not provide students with many opportunities at creating discourse. And eloquent style per se was not likely taught by teachers whose most advanced study of rhetoric consisted, as often was the case, of perhaps one composition course in college. The result was too many inarticulate people, unsure of their abilities to phrase their ideas well and to deliver their statements capably.

People no longer able to articulate well their hopes and fears for the future turn to, and confer leadership upon, capable communicators who act as surrogate spokespersons for members of society now mute. This phenomenon was recognized, and capitalized upon rhetorically, by Richard Nixon during his 1968 presidential campaign. Many voters responded favorably to his characterization of them as a "Great Silent Majority," willing to accept his leadership founded upon ability to articulate well the hopes and fears of Americans for the future. In far too many speeches that occur now, speakers truthfully admit at the outset, "Unaccustomed as I am to public speaking. . . ."

Perhaps many erstwhile speakers are inhibited as well by a feeling (at some level of awareness) that one person's discourse on but one occasion is unlikely to change the course of events. After all, attitudes and actions most likely are molded by a matrix of message inputs, many of which are "unorganized" and "overlaid" to form that earlier mentioned, complex communication "mosaic," which "consists of an immense number of fragments or bits of information on an immense number of topics . . . scattered over time and space and modes of communication. Each individual must grasp from this mosaic those bits which serve his needs, must group them into message sets which are relevant for him at any given time . . . and close the gaps between them in order to arrive at a coherent picture of the world to which he can respond." So persuasion to attitudes or actions rarely results from "any one communication encounter, or even a series of encounters by a single speaker or writer."[11]

But one speech, at a pivotal point in time, *can* alter the course of events! In Tokyo, Japan, on the evening of August 23, 1950, grim-faced men met in the sixth-floor conference room of the Dai Ichi Building, General Douglas MacArthur's headquarters. The Korean War was going badly for the United States; military disaster was imminent. Retreats often became routs; "bug out" entered GI jargon to signify fleeing in disorder; successive defense lines disintegrated as Americans were pushed south down the Korean peninsula into a small perimeter around the port city of Pusan for a desperate "Custer's Last Stand." As supreme commander, MacArthur planned an audacious counter-attack: an amphibious landing by Marines at Inchon, on the west coast of Korea near Seoul, about 150 miles behind the rear of communist troops surrounding Pusan.

But Inchon was anathema in Washington, D.C. The tidal range of nearly 32 feet was among the highest in the world. LSTs (Landing Ship, Tank) required 29 feet of water, but high tide lasted only two to three hours. After unloading troops and equipment, LSTs could be stranded on mud flats until the next high tide; and with insufficient numbers available in the U.S. Navy, 37 LSTs (some smelling "vividly of fish") were leased from the Japanese merchant service. Inchon had no beaches, so smaller landing craft needed engines to keep bows against seawalls 12 to 14 feet high while Marines scaled them on makeshift wooden ladders. With evening high tide at 7:20 P.M., Marines had 27 minutes of daylight to secure a city the size of Omaha—with no reinforcements until the next high tide.

In Washington, D.C., the Joint Chiefs of Staff were worried. So Army Chief of Staff General Lawton Collins and Chief of Naval Operations Admiral Forrest Sherman flew to Tokyo to *dissuade* MacArthur from Inchon. For the first 80 minutes of that pivotal conference, Admiral James Doyle's briefing detailed disadvantages of the landing site, and General Collins immediately suggested an alternative site farther south, which was seconded by Admiral Sherman. MacArthur then spoke, uninterrupted, for approximately 30 minutes. Collins and Sherman changed their minds and endorsed Inchon to President Truman. On September 15, 1950, the First Marine Division landed at Inchon. The operation was eminently successful. By September 23, the North Korean army around Pusan was in full retreat; by September 28, Seoul was recaptured and restored to the South Korean government; and by October 20, Americans crossed the 38th parallel and captured the North Korean capital of Pyongyang. By November 23, virtually all of North Korea had fallen and American armed forces were within a few miles of the Yalu River border of Red China. All of this happened because Douglas MacArthur spoke persuasively. History as we know it today was changed by a single speech.[12]

Most speakers today are unlikely to achieve a singular success equal to that of MacArthur's that evening. Because of that vast communication "mosaic" today, speakers more likely will exert another kind of influence at a given point in time because of another phenomenon identified in empirical research about communication and persuasion—opinion leadership. Another truism warrants repetition: "When people are exposed to information which they believe is important, they will generally turn to additional sources to verify or supplement what they got from the original source."[13] With their effectiveness enhanced by prowess with word choice and word arrangement, public speakers have the potential to become those "additional sources" to whom people turn.

Consistently, people are "crucially influenced in many matters" by individuals perceived as "opinion leaders" amidst a matrix of what is read or heard as discourse. Several factors conduce to achieving opinion leadership. One criterion for exerting influence often is similarity; but because a group's opinion leader typically is deemed as better informed about the matter at hand, a more significant criterion is knowledge.

In many instances of influence through oral discourse, a speaker becomes "a super representative" of a group because of being "characteristically more competent," with "access to wider sources of pertinent information." Furthermore, when "found to be 'like everyone else, only slightly more so' in reference to group norms," an opinion leader's "influence is related . . . to the *personification of certain values* of the group to which leader and follower belong" and "for a considerable number" of other individuals as well. Although many studies of this phenomenon sought to measure "the leader's role in producing change," the effect more often ascertained was "influence in favor of constancy and reinforcement"; and this guidance from opinion leaders "seems to be sought or accepted in specific areas partly—or perhaps largely—because it provides . . . followers with the sort of satisfactions they seek in those areas."[14] Viewed from another perspective, opinion leaders are those persons capable of phrasing well and thereby reinforcing attitudinal leanings that audiences have acquired from myriad other messages and information that compose the vast communication mosaic in which those Americans now live. To become that opinion leader as a result of effective speaking requires the artistry to produce the best words in their best orders.

Admiration for artistry, as a practical goal in discourse, is a persistent notion in rhetorical theory. As the consummate orator himself, Cicero extolled sentences "marked by a certain artistry and polish," which in turn would produce "applause and admiration." He added that "although we hope to win a 'Bravo, capital' as often as possible . . . the actual ejaculation 'Couldn't be better!' is the one I should like to hear frequently." Cicero also observed pragmatically that "when a citizen hears an able orator, he readily credits what is said; he imagines everything to be true, he believes and relishes the force of it; and in short, the persuasive language of the speaker wins his absolute, his hearty assent." Moreover, that impact was not only upon learned people, sensitive to nuances of eloquence, but also upon "unlearned" audiences because "everybody is able to discriminate between what is right and wrong in matters of art and proportion by a sort of subconscious instinct, without having any theory of art or proportion of their own."[15] For speakers who would achieve the status of opinion leaders today through oral discourse, is their prowess with words any less likely to exert the same degree of influence? After all, whether as "sound bites" on the evening news or simply words that linger in the consciousness of audiences amid that "immense number of fragments or bits of information on an immense number of topics," these are precisely the sentences that allow people to "close the gaps" and "arrive at a coherent picture of the world."

ELOQUENCE

Assume that a monument will be built in Washington, D.C., to honor John F. Kennedy. When monuments to prominent people are built in our capitol city, three items often are engraved thereon: names of those individuals, dates of their births and deaths, and some words penned or uttered by them and linked inescapably with their names. At the Lincoln Memorial, he is sculpted seated—with the Gettysburg Address engraved nearby; at Thomas Jefferson's memorial near the Tidal Basin, a statue has him standing in the middle of the Rotunda—with words he wrote engraved around the dome overhead. And *if* a similar monument is built to honor John F. Kennedy, we *know* what words from him would be engraved thereon: "Ask not what your country can do for you—ask what you can do for your country."

Those words were uttered in John Kennedy's inaugural address on January 20, 1961. In all probability, their polished form is, to an appreciable extent, the product of Kennedy's speechwriter, Ted Sorensen (Sorensen's debate coach at the University of Nebraska, Donald Olson, once told me that even as an undergraduate, Sorensen extemporized sentences during debates in forms similar to those he would write for Kennedy years later). Regardless of who authored their final form, however, those words are linked inescapably with Kennedy, and they most likely would appear on any memorial to him. Suppose, however, that the eminently quotable statement had appeared in the inaugural address exactly the way its argument was phrased earlier for a campaign speech in Cadillac Square, Detroit, on Labor Day, September 6, 1960: "The new frontier is not what I promise I am going to do for you. The new frontier is what I ask you to do for your country." That statement would not be engraved on any monument, for it is colloquial, if not banal. Thus, although the Detroit statement has the same content as the inaugural address argument, its form is different—and deficient. Functional eloquence is missing, for nothing warrants, "notice me, remember me, carry me around in your memory for a generation." So *how* something is said can make a significant difference. The pivotal variable is the style in discourse.

Style is a troublesome word. The term is used in various ways, to designate modes of dress or hair grooming or salient characteristics of virtually any endeavors in which choice is exercised. For style in discourse, however, the word has a precise meaning. Whether discourse is several sentences in length or hundreds or more sentences in length, essential tasks are choosing words (lexicon) and arranging them in appropriate orders (syntax). Our sentences are constrained, however, by the common idiom, whereby word choices and their arrangements conform to customary usage learned by people using that particular language. Indeed, our language habits are organized into *"hierarchies of alternatives"*; for "at both lexical and structural choice points, to the extent that there *is* choice, certain alternatives will be most probable, others less probable, and others very improbable." So *"style is defined as an individual's deviations from norms . . . these deviations being in the statistical properties of those structural features for which there exists some degree of choice in his code."* Thus, style evolves from *"how* a person talks about something" more so than *"what* he talks about."[16] After all, John Kennedy's more idiomatic statement in Detroit during the presidential campaign of 1960 had essentially the same content as the most quoted line from his inaugural address. But form for the inaugural address embodied eloquent style, which accounted for its rhetorical power. What remains is to demonstrate how substantive content articulated with eloquent form of the best words in their best orders may achieve similar impact.

Ask several people to tell you the first six words of Abraham Lincoln's Gettysburg Address. Most likely they easily will recall "Four score and seven years ago." Then, ask those people when they last heard or read those six words. For many people, the last exposure to those six words was many years ago, perhaps a decade or longer. But they still know the words. That is memorability! Suppose Lincoln began the Gettysburg Address by saying "Eighty-seven years ago." In that common idiom, content is exactly the same, but few would remember the line. Nor could people remember the line as someone humorously conceived it might have been uttered in a manner thought characteristic of President Dwight Eisenhower (who, although immensely popular, was not particularly admired for his prowess with the English language): "I haven't checked the figures but eighty-seven years ago, I think it was . . . ." Or the line could have been uttered in a form similar to that which some people deemed characteristic of President Jimmy Carter: "Exactly two hundred and one years, five months and one day ago, our forefathers—and our foremothers, too, as my wife, the First Lady, reminds me—our highly competent Founding Persons brought forth on this land mass a new nation, or entity. . . ." Lincoln's lexicon *is* better.

Americans today rarely write with Abraham Lincoln's eloquence. Suppose he were a student in a composition class in this country during the latter part of the twentieth century. Had he turned in his Gettysburg Address as an essay, a teacher would have looked at the first six words and likely written in the margin, "Say what you mean," and in all probability, young Abe would have received a C-minus grade for his efforts. For he would have deviated from the customary idiom for word choice. "Four score and seven" is archaic language from an earlier time (although in the 1860s, when people were readily familiar with the scriptures, "score" was not as much a deviation from familiar usage as a reference for 20).

The same principle about lexical departure from the common idiom holds true for syntax or word arrangement. In English, we are taught to write actor–action sentences wherein subjects of sentences occur before predicates and objects follow predicates. If the King James Bible had been written favoring that normative placement, the Ephesians should have said "Diana is great" when referring to the goddess they admired, for this arrangement is subject-predicate-object syntax. But in the version according to St. Paul, their statement was "Great is Diana." For customary placements of the kernel elements in a sentence can be inverted syntactically to an object-predicate-subject sentence, a "scheme" of inversion known in traditional rhetoric handbooks as *anastrophe*. (A "scheme" is a plan or format for accomplishing a desired objective; the term is used extensively in rhetorical theory to designate syntactical patterns conducive to persuasive eloquence; and hereafter in this book, *scheme* is used with that precise operational definition.) And although the three words are exactly the same, the *e*ffect and *a*ffect from their uncommon arrangement is different. Somehow, with "Great is Diana," that goddess *is* greater and the statement more emphatic.

Americans no longer learn those schemes and other stylistic options as part of training for composition that undergirds effective speaking. One reason is the cumbersome Greek and Latin terminology by which those language conformations were known. In the English Renaissance, though, students were taught nearly 200 exotic names for stylistic maneuvers, such as *antimetabole, brachiepia, epizeuxis, sinathrismus, zeugma,* and other arcane terminology to describe a "garden of eloquence" deemed desirable then. Moreover, diligent students in that era would have mastered those stylistic features in their writing, for ideally educated gentlemen (in those days such learning likely was not for women) were as deft with a pen as with a sword. Shakespeare was a product of that educational system; and the Bard incorporated virtually all of those stylistic features throughout his writing and thereby undoubtedly enhanced the impress of his discourse. Yet Renaissance students also were confronted with imprecise if not nebulous ways of describing functional effects of style in discourse upon the psychology of respondents. Why strive for "vivacity" or "sublimity" if the behavioral response is neither known nor understood? As the critic and theorist I. A. Richards observed, "the interesting question is surely NOT whether Shakespeare uses a given figure, but what *that* variation from flat writing does for him and for us just there."[17] Thus, an essential goal of this book is to explain how style can be used to advantage now by public speakers who must communicate effectively in the world of pragmatic affairs.

We easily remember "four score and seven years ago," but why? Bob Newhart had a humorous explanation. Before starring in television situation comedies, he was a successful stand-up comic whose monologues were recorded as "The Button-Down Mind of Bob Newhart," and in one he played the Madison Avenue public relations man hired by Abraham Lincoln as a speechwriter. An angry Lincoln telephoned his highly paid speechwriter to complain about a draft submitted for a public statement from the president when a cemetery would be dedicated at Gettysburg. Did the speechwriter really want Lincoln to say, "Four score and seven years ago," while standing on a platform in public? The Madison Avenue response was "That's a grabber." Yes, those words "grabbed" Americans sufficiently well to be carried around in their heads for years, if not decades. But a quality of language that "grabs" is no more precise and hence capable of emulation than that which is sublime or vivacious. Another perspective is helpful.

In a large shopping mall, numerous business establishments compete for attention, hoping people will look at their windows and be enticed into the store. One of those windows displays this sign:

ƧALE

If that stimulus is in the periphery of shoppers' vision, they likely will orient perceptually toward it. Even if they glance for only a split second, that place of business has won half its battle. People *did* look at that window rather than others competing for their attention. The operative factor was novelty. Although the word *novel* often connotes something trivial (prizes children got in Crackerjack boxes were called novelties), perceptual psychologists appreciate this factor differently.

In the psychology of communication, novelty is one of those "factors of advantage" or "stimulus attributes commanding priority." Novelty evolves from "a *discrepancy* between the individual's expectancy about the stimulus and his present perception of that stimulus." Thus, we expect that in a sign announcing a "SALE," the letter *S* will be printed correctly. *S* printed in reverse is discrepant with expectations and hence endowed with novelty.

Many people remember a television commercial of several years ago. A sleepy-eyed man, unshaven and dressed in a bathrobe, opens the door of the medicine chest on his bathroom wall; it opens into the next apartment; and someone from the next apartment unexpectedly confronts him smiling broadly, waving, and saying, "Hi guy." A medicine chest on the bathroom wall opening into the next apartment is discrepant with expectations. The commercial embodied novelty and attracted viewers' attention to the product presented, an underarm deodorant. Substantial research demonstrates the capability of novelty to arouse a psychological drive to pay close attention, and "the view that unfamiliar stimulus objects are approached, explored, and manipulated rests upon a variety of well-authenticated observations." Moreover, as an axiom in communication contexts, "in ordinary speech, we attend to an unusual event rather than a simultaneous usual event" because a "filter" in the human nervous system has a "bias" toward the novel stimulus, which therefore is "more likely to elicit a response."[18]

The same attentional factor of advantage can function at subtle levels of syntax and lexicon. Audiences expect a speaker's words to be in the customary, familiar idiom; people also expect them to be arranged in habitual patterns taught to us throughout our education. So word choice (lexicon) that deviates from the common idiom, such as Lincoln's "four score and seven," is as novel as the word arrangement (syntax) that deviates from the common idiom, such as "Great is Diana." And psychologists agree about something else: the more that people pay attention to any stimulus, the greater the likelihood that it will be learned and remembered. In the psychology of communication, that effect is known as *emphasis*, which persuasion and learning theorists value as a "significant influence upon the learning and remembering process."

> A general principle is that the stronger or more potent the stimulus, the greater impress it will make upon the responding person. The best omnibus word to describe this principle in operation is *emphasis*, the special stress or weight given to particular stimuli. In the communication situation this means the emphasis given to particular stimulus units (whole arguments, propositional sentences, key words) by presenting them with special potency.[19]

Familiar ways of achieving emphasis are increases in volume for oral discourse or larger print for written discourse. This book, however, is primarily about stylistic skills by which sentences are cast eloquently to increase the likelihood of their being noticed and remembered to exert influence among all other statements composing a communication mosaic.

For all of the contemporary research that corroborates the power of words to be quotable, memorable, and prepotent for persuasion, the same outlook pervaded the theory advanced by pragmatic and perceptive classical rhetoricians. Aristotle's *Rhetoric* (1404b) observed that "words are like men; as we feel a difference between people from afar and our fellow townsmen, so it is with our feeling for language. And hence it is well to give the ordinary idiom an air of remoteness; the hearers are struck by what is out of the way, and like what strikes them." Or, as another translator rendered this passage, "to alter or vary language in this way invests it with a higher dignity; for we feel towards language just as we feel towards men; 'familiarity breeds contempt' for the words we are constantly meeting in everyday intercourse, whilst 'strangers' assume a higher importance and dignity in our eyes. Hence we are to aim at a 'strange' *i.e.,* unusual, not familiar, novel, out of the common way diction" because with "uncommon" style that "strikes one as singular," communicators can attain a statement that "forces itself upon the attention."[20]

Effective communicators, whether in writing or in speaking, want that attention whereby their words, phrases, and sentences have advantages for being noticed and remembered in the vast communication mosaic of today. People cannot recall all the words intended for them no matter how hard they might try to pay attention. For at any given moment, a welter of stimuli likely are present to people who must select those to which they will respond in some unified, coherent way; yet "only a small portion become part of actual experience; and that portion is not a random sample of what is objectively available." What we *do* respond to is the result of attention, "the active, selective aspect of perception, involving the preparation and orientation of the individual to perceive a particular stimulus pattern"—with "consequent inhibition of all others."[21] And people are persuaded primarily by those messages to which they pay attention.

With novelty as its determining factor of attention, emphasis derived from style or form of a statement can supplement the substance or content of a message to help assure that it becomes a salient stimulus. Perhaps not all sentences in discourse merit emphasis from stylistically derived novelty. But prowess with language surely should enhance key arguments or summary statements. These are the opinion leader's sentences that ideally might become the persuasive morals and maxims that ultimately influence people's behavior. Of course *all* sentences in a specific discourse actually could embody some source of style and not seem affected or obtrusive. After all, every sentence in Lincoln's Gettysburg Address incorporates at least one deviation from the common idiom as a source of style (some sentences have three!), and the speech is an exemplar of eloquence that any public speaker might hope to attain today.

Simply reading about eloquence, however, is insufficient. You must do things, too. A story is told about a Japanese pilot during World War II. He belonged to a Kamikaze unit, whose pilots were to load their aircraft with bombs and fly out to where an American fleet was located. Kamikaze pilots would pick out an American ship, preferably an aircraft carrier, and dive their planes into it—suicidally dying in the explosion, but they hoped, sinking that vessel. To become more effective with language, you must not be like that Kamikaze pilot who flew 17 missions: he was interested in the program but not truly involved. To acquire prowess whereby public speakers use the best words in their best orders, involvement is mandatory. When asked in this book to practice with specific sources of style for effective discourse, do it. Only that way can you come and read about how words work—and go with confidence and capabilities as an eloquent stylist. So in some other words from John Kennedy's inaugural address, "Let us begin."

NOTES

1. See my more complete discussion of this situation in "The Symbolic Substance of Style in Presidential Discourse," *Style* 16 (1982): 38–49.

2. Samuel Becker, "Rhetorical Studies for the Modern World," in *The Prospect of Rhetoric*, ed. Lloyd Bitzer and Edwin Black (Englewood Cliffs: Prentice-Hall, 1971): 27, 33.

3. Father Walter J. Ong, *Orality and Literacy: The Technologizing of the Word* (London: Methuen, 1982): 5, 7–8, 31–32.

4. Ong, 72.

5. Ong, 72–73, 136.

6. Ong, 74.

7. Donald C. Bryant, *Rhetorical Dimensions in Criticism* (Baton Rouge, LA: Louisiana State University Press, 1973): 11, 19. Or see

Bryant's "Rhetoric: Its Functions and Scope," *Quarterly Journal of Speech* 39 (December 1953): 401–424.

8. Roderick Hart and Don Burks, "Rhetorical Sensitivity and Social Interaction," *Speech Monographs* 39 (June 1972): 75–91.

9. Andrew T. Weaver and Ordean G. Ness, *The Fundamentals and Forms of Speech* (New York: Odyssey, 1957): 10–11. See also Jon Eisenson, J. Jeffery Auer, and John V. Irwin, *The Psychology of Communication* (New York: Appleton-Century-Crofts, 1963): 5–6. For a compelling discussion (and sometimes graphic depiction) of how stimuli evoke only what is in the brain already, see Wilder Penfield and Lamar Roberts, *Speech and Brain Mechanisms* (Princeton: Princeton University Press, 1959).

10. After Lloyd F. Bitzer, "The Rhetorical Situation," *Philosophy and Rhetoric* 1 (Winter 1968): 1–14.

11. Becker, 22–25, 33.

12. My research about this rhetorical success used primary source materials, such as correspondence and oral histories, in the Douglas MacArthur Archives (Norfolk, VA), the Marine Corps Museum and Archives (Washington D.C.), and the U.S. Naval War College (Newport, RI). The results of my research are reported in "General Douglas MacArthur's Oratory on Behalf of Inchon: Discourse that Altered the Course of History," *Southern Communication Journal* 58 (Fall 1992): 1–12; and, with Bernard K. Duffy as coauthor, *Douglas MacArthur, Warrior as Wordsmith* (Westport, CT: Greenwood, 1997).

13. Becker, 35.

14. See Joseph T. Klapper, *The Effects of Mass Communication* (New York: Free Press, 1960): 34–36, 51; Elihu Katz, "The Two-Step Flow of Communication: An Up-To-Date Report on an Hypothesis," *Public Opinion Quarterly* 21 (1957): 63, 77; Elihu Katz and Paul F. Lazarsfeld, *Personal Influence: The Part Played by People in the Flow of Mass Communication* (Glencoe, IL: Free Press, 1955): 286; and Bernard Berelson and Gary Steiner, *Human Behavior: An Inventory of Scientific Findings* (New York: Harcourt, Brace, and World, 1964): 550.

15. See Cicero *Brutus* 14 and 50; also *De Oratore* i. 12.50 and 33.152 as well as iii. 26.101 and 50.195.

16. Charles Osgood, "Some Effects of Motivation on Style of Encoding," in *Style in Language*, ed. Thomas A. Sebeok (New York: John Wiley and Sons and the Massachusetts Institute of Technology, 1960): 293–296.

17. I. A. Richards, *Speculative Instruments* (Chicago: University of Chicago Press, 1955): 158.

18. My discussion here is based on Eisenson, Auer, and Irwin, 239; William N. Dember, *The Psychology of Perception* (New York: Holt, Rinehart and Winston, 1960): 348; D. E. Berlyne, "Novelty and Curiosity as Determinants of Exploratory Behavior," *British Journal of Psychology* 40

(1949): 68–80; Judson S. Brown, *The Motivation of Behavior* (New York: McGraw-Hill, 1961): 330; Donald E. Broadbent, *Perception and Communication* (London: Pergamon Press, 1958): 85–86.

19. Eisenson, Auer, and Irwin, 250.

20. See the Lane Cooper translation of Aristotle's *Rhetoric* iii. 2 (New York: Appleton-Century-Crofts, 1932) and E. M. Cope's translation of the same passage in *An Introduction to Aristotle's Rhetoric* (London: MacMillan, 1867): 283–284.

21. A host of psychologists attest to the role of attention, such as Edwin G. Boring, Herbert S. Langfeld, and Henry Porter Weld, *Foundations of Psychology* (New York: John Wiley and Sons, 1948): 218; Bernard Berelson and Gary A. Steiner, *Human Behavior: An Inventory of Scientific Findings* (New York: Harcourt, Brace, and World, 1964): 100; Karl U. Smith and William M. Smith, *The Behavior of Man* (New York: Henry Holt, 1958): 233; George A. Miller, *Psychology: The Science of Mental Life* (New York: Harper and Row, 1962): 346.

2 ANTITHESES EVERYWHERE

A main difference between poet and poet, orator and orator, really does lie in the aptness with which they arrange their words.

Dionysius of Halicarnassus, *On Literary Composition*

Many people remember these words: "One small step for [a] man—one giant leap for mankind." Neil Armstrong uttered them in 1969 when he stepped on the moon. The occasion was momentous; Americans paid close attention to their television sets; the words have been repeated and reprinted since then. But many people remember the line even though they read or heard it only a few times, long ago. Neil Armstrong did not make up the statement as he came down the ladder. According to one version, NASA commissioned the line to be written for him by James Dickey, a poet laureate. And in all likelihood, Armstrong's line for posterity was printed out on his sleeve with a magic marker or laundry pencil so that he just might glance at his arm while holding the ladder, descending, and reading it aloud into the helmet microphone. For that momentous deed, accompanying words had to be uttered accurately. This chapter explains how and why those words in that order were so memorable and quotable. By learning and practicing the precepts explained in the following pages, your statements can have similar advantage for

memorability and quotability. This source of functionally eloquent style is called *antithesis*.

THE ESSENCE OF ANTITHESIS

To understand the power of antithesis, try this experiment
with several people. Tell your subjects that you want to play a
word game. You will say three words quickly in immediate
succession. After you have said the third word and clapped
your hands, your subjects in this experiment must write down
immediately whatever other *one* word *first* popped into their
minds after your sequence of three words. Tell people to play
the game honestly and not try to "psych out" the intent of
the experiment. You want to know the one word—and only
one word—that is their instantaneous response after hearing
your three words. As the first three words, quickly say *devil,
dark,* and *sinister.* The likely response will be a word compatible in meaning, or even a synonym for one of your words,
such as *Satan, evil,* or *Hell.* Your subjects are unlikely to
respond with a fourth word that is opposite in meaning, such
as *good* or *angel.* Using *hot, sweaty,* and *sultry,* try the same
experiment with those same people as your subjects. *Cold* or
jacket are unlikely responses, for most people will say a fourth
word such as *sun, beach,* or *Florida.*

Once a context is formed by words with compatible
meanings, someone is not likely to come up with a next word
that is semantically incompatible, if not opposite, in meaning. This psychological constraint constantly influences composition when casting sentences as writers or as speakers. The
preference for words compatible in meaning to be placed
close together operates "automatically and unconsciously" in
language behavior, and words used early in sentences exert a
cumulative, psychological pressure to select successive words
that are similar in their meanings to the ones chosen for the

beginnings of those statements.[1] So the common idiom is characterized by sentences wherein words that are compatible in meaning are positioned close together syntactically. Therefore, these are the sentences that people *expect* when they hear and read discourse. But someone may deviate from that normative syntax of the common idiom and arrange words with opposite meanings in close proximity syntactically within a sentence; when this happens, the sentence is discrepant with expectations and endowed with novelty as a factor of attention. This sentence mode embodies a source of style known as antithesis (the plural is *antitheses*). In discourse that has endured the test of time for persuasive memorability and quotability, antitheses are ubiquitous.

Admittedly, early languages often had words that within themselves bore opposite meanings. For instance, some Egyptian hieroglyphics embodied opposites, such as symbols signifying good–bad, high–low, give–take, bring–send, hill–dale, up–down, or with–without. In their later languages, however, people tended to opt for positive statements more than ones embodying negatives, for "there is far more involvement and interest in information which asserts or implies that something is so than in information which denies that something is so." Indeed, "in most kinds of discourse (with the probable exception of legal documents, regulations, *etc.*) affirmative statements are more frequent than negative ones." Because of "interest in positive information, its frequency of use, and the emphasis given to it in early conceptual learning," people typically avoid stating the opposites, or negatives, necessary to make an antithesis. While analyzing antitheses such as "to be a blessing, and *not a curse*" or "The one shall be taken, and *the other left*," Alexander Bain observed, "It is the prevailing habit of language to express only one term of these couples and to leave the other to be implied or understood. . . . When we call a line 'straight,' we might also say it is not crooked, but generally leave this to be mentally supplied." So antithesis evolves from "explicitly stating the contrast implied in the very meaning of a term or fact," and this "full statement of the opposite, or obverse, side of a feeling or a fact" constitutes "a departure from the common form of language, which is content with naming one side alone."[2] So to make antitheses, communicators must expend psychological energy to state what would have been unstated opposites, and their sentences must do so with balance and symmetry as well as other functional attributes.

HOW ANTITHESES ARE MADE

Some antitheses result from positioning antonyms close together syntactically within a sentence. Antonyms are those two words—and only two words—that are accepted as direct opposites of one another, such as *hot* and *cold, love* and *hate, war* and *peace, long* and *short, fast* and *slow,* or *high* and *low.* The closer the antonyms are placed within that sentence, the sharper and more epigrammatic the antithesis. In his inaugural address, John Kennedy used a double antithesis made from two sets of antonyms: "If a free society cannot help the *many* who are *poor* how can it save the *few* who are *rich.*" His stylistic predilection for antitheses may have had origins in childhood experiences, for his mother, Rose, taught the Kennedy children epigrams such as "Promptness is a compliment to the intelligent and a rebuke to the stupid." Of course President Kennedy found a totally empathetic speechwriter in Ted Sorensen.

Antitheses founded upon antonyms in proximity are particularly advantageous because people responding to communication may prefer "binary comparisons." After all, antonyms are "a very important class of words, playing a more practical (sorting) function than synonyms. We have many word pairs which suggest that we like to make binary comparisons, that this forms part of our thinking habits:

high–low, hot–cold, good–evil, war–peace, rich–poor." Experimental research in psycholinguistics corroborates this assumption. Investigating reaction times for similarity and difference, researchers measured the speed with which people responded to a single stimulus word by supplying another word. Four classifications for response words prevailed: general identification, such as *kill–destroy;* specific identification, such as *ocean–Pacific;* contingent relation, such as *lake–boat,* and essential contrast or opposition, such as *black–white.* Mean reaction time, in seconds, for words showing contrast or opposition was 1.104; for general identification, 1.344; for contingent relation, 1.442; and for specific identification, 1.516. Thus, respondents' "fastest time is for direct contrast" because "contrasting or differentiating is easier and more natural than identifying."[3] Although uncommon and thereby deviations from the common idiom, neatly balanced antitheses from juxtaposed antonyms are eloquent. They also are eminently practical for achieving efficient responses, confirming Aristotle's recommendation of these schemes "because things are best known when opposites are put side by side."[4]

Another type of antithesis is derived from juxtaposing words or phrases that mean the opposite although they are not antonyms, specifically. President Kennedy characterized his inauguration not as a "victory of party" but rather a "celebration of freedom." Whereas a "victory of party" is self–serving if not ignoble, a "celebration of freedom" is more altruistic. Similarly, he lauded those rights of man that did not come from "the generosity of the state" but from "the hand of God." Again, the two phrases have differing meanings suggestive of opposites. Richard Nixon made the same kind of antithesis in his acceptance address to the 1968 Republican Convention: "Let us accept this challenge, not as a grim duty, but as an exciting adventure" or "After an era of confrontation the time has come for an era of negotiation."[5] In both cases, Nixon contrasts a basically negative notion with one of positive value. Following this trend in presidential discourse, Bill Clinton offered an antithesis in his first inaugural address: "We will act—with peaceful diplomacy whenever possible, with force when necessary." Or as Martin Luther King, Jr., said in his "I Have a Dream" speech, "With this faith we will be able to transform the jangling discords of our nation into a beautiful symphony of brotherhood."

MASTERING THE FORM

Antitheses are difficult to master at first. They are not made by starting from the first word of a sentence and adding the second, third, fourth, fifth words and so on. The cumulative, psychological context of early words will exert pressure to come up with successive words that are similar or compatible in meaning rather than opposite; and that psychological constraint likely is operative to greater extent when people are forming sentences while speaking. So draw a see-saw or teeter-totter.

▲

Next, pick two opposites, preferably antonyms at first, and put one on each side of the see-saw:

best   worst

▲

Then—and only then—write the remainder of the sentence in and around your two opposites to create a relatively short, "balanced" statement, which has approximately the same number of words on one side of the fulcrum as on the other. Again, the key word is *balance*. You may remember the antithesis that goes with those antonyms in close proximity:

<u>It was the best of times; it was the worst of times.</u>
▲

Did you remember that opening sentence by Charles Dickens in *A Tale of Two Cities?* If so, you can appreciate how antitheses contribute to quotability and memorability—even decades later!

The key to making antitheses is to use the see-saw or teeter–totter technique. Several years ago, I was informed— about 45 minutes before the event—that I was expected to make a brief speech during the dinner party celebrating my parents' 50th wedding anniversary. I immediately found some paper and began to draw some see-saws. My parents were married in 1933 during the depths of the Great Depression, so on one side of the teeter-totter, I wrote "cold," "dark," and "Depression." If you were helping me write that speech, what three words would go on the other side of the see-saw to balance those off and form the basis of an epigram about how their lives changed? Try making that sentence now.

<u>cold   dark   Depression</u>
▲

HELPFUL HINT *As you draft formal statements to be read or heard, be on the lookout for a possible pair of antonyms. If you used the word* new, *stop and draw a see-saw. Put* new *on one side and* old *on the other. Then, see if your subject matter lends itself to a balanced antithesis. Similarly, your use of* freedom, *for example, should trigger an antithesis with* oppression, *or a sentence that embodies early the word* slow *should cause you to pause and create an antithesis using* fast. *Essentially, you will state what normally would have been that unstated opposite.*

Applying this principle of balance, some people made these lines in their first tries during one of my workshop–seminars on style: "We are so good at making war and so bad at keeping peace" or "Our first kiss was so sweet and our final good-bye was so bitter." The first sentence is a double antithesis, because it has two sets of opposites; the second sentence is a triple antithesis!

Rule to Remember

The best antitheses are *balanced*, with approximately the same number of words on one side of the "fulcrum" as on the obverse side.

To practice this principle, balance the following antithesis from Bill Clinton's acceptance address to the 1992 Democratic Convention: "And yet just as we have won the cold war abroad, we are losing the battles for economic opportunity and social justice here at home." Yes, *won* is counterbalanced by *losing; abroad* is counterbalanced by *at home*; but *cold war* is offset by *battles* for BOTH *economic opportunity* and *social justice*. Noting that *cold* has an opposite, a better balanced antithesis might be, for instance, "We have won the cold war for political democracy abroad but are losing the heated battle for economic opportunity at home."

When diagrammed as a see-saw or teeter-totter, an antithesis should not look like either of these two drawings:

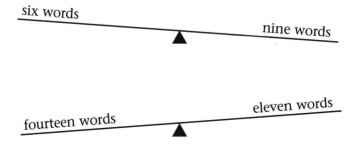

In both cases, visual renderings of the number of words in each half of the antithesis reveal how the sentences are not balanced with the symmetry conducive to quotable epigrams. To test your understanding of this concept, which of the following antitheses has the most symmetry from balancing opposites?

A. After this initial defeat we seek ultimate peace.
B. After this defeat we seek victory and ultimate peace.
C. After this initial defeat in war we seek ultimate victory in peace.
D. After initial defeat we seek ultimate peace.
E. After defeat in war we seek ultimate victory and lasting peace.

The correct answer is C. Again, *balance* is a key word to describe the best antitheses.

As another desideratum, antitheses should not "belabor the obvious," such as "It was not a hard task but an easy one" or "He had a lot of money, not a little." A task that is not hard must be easy, and obviously so; a person with a lot of money obviously does not have a little amount. Those sentences insult respondents' intelligence, and their reaction also might be one of suspicion because the communicator apparently is trying to make the proverbial mountain out of a molehill.

Try making a double antithesis *now* about some current issue in which you are interested. In the space below, pick two sets of opposites first, place them on either sides of the see–saw, then write the remainder of the sentence in between and around them to come up with a balanced, relatively short statement with approximately the same number of words in one half as in the other.

▲

When casting the above antithesis, the word *but* likely appears directly over the fulcrum of the see-saw and enhances the dichotomy inherent in the conformation.

Another key to making antitheses is to develop an inner eye or ear for opposites—and take advantage of opportunities that arise during composition of statements. For example, I was involved in one campaign not as a speechwriter but as a media relations person, handling all statements to the press from an organization on one side of a referendum issue. The morning newspaper had carried a story from the other side about all of the wonderful things that would happen if its point of view prevailed in the coming election. I was sitting in my office when a newspaper reporter telephoned and invited me to respond from the perspective of my organization. I immediately created the impression that someone was with me and that a conference was in progress. I told him I would call him back in a few minutes. Actually, I was sitting at my desk alone, with a third cup of coffee to get me awake for the rest of the day; but from the instant the reporter asked for a response, I was very busy—planning and writing out sentences before calling him back. I was heeding some friendly advice that I should not say things to the media off the top of my head. In my mind, a potential antithesis resides in what is promised as opposed to what is delivered. I drew my see-saw:

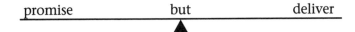

promise   but   deliver

I recalled a drawing showing two, well-dressed gentlemen with attaché cases, standing on a street corner in Manhattan. The sign said "Wall Street," so they presumably were Republican bankers. Both were looking up at a piece of pie flying over Manhattan, and the one said to the other, "Look, another Democratic campaign promise." For "pie in the sky" symbolizes unrealistic and grandiose expectations, and the following antithesis began to take form:

They promise pie in the sky but

After the fulcrum word of *but* and then *deliver,* a counterbalance was needed for "pie in the sky." I initially opted for *baloney,* but that was only one word to counterbalance four words in "pie in the sky." So I created the following sentence:

They promise pie in the sky but deliver baloney on cracked wheat.

After making several other antitheses, I called the reporter back and worked them in during my statement. As the interview concluded, he asked if I had said, "They promise pie in the sky but deliver baloney on cracked wheat." The sentence was quoted in the news story the next day. The moral is simple: well-cast antitheses increase the odds that sentences will be noticed, perhaps to become "sound bites" for the evening news on television, and even be memorable and quotable later.

Consider court trials, for example. In high-profile cases, jurors likely hear thousands upon thousands of words from defense and prosecution attorneys (plus myriad words from various witnesses). The result is a communication mosaic of considerable magnitude. The exact words that jurors remember in the jury room, while making their decision, just might match an attorney's exact words—and only words—that were quoted directly in the newspapers the day after. One heated exchange took place during a high-profile case, when an Army drill instructor stood accused of rape. The prosecutor had made the point (to which the judge agreed) that drill sergeants have so much power over trainees that they do not need to use a weapon or threaten force to be guilty of rape. The defense attorney in turn retorted, "Are trainees so ignorant that they can't distinguish between a drill sergeant telling them to run up a hill or lie down on a bed?" That antithesis between "run up a hill or lie down on a bed" *was* the pivotal part of the only passage quoted directly in the Associated Press wire service account of the legal proceedings that day.[6] Again, antitheses have an edge for quotability!

"THE RULE" OF RECENCY

Making effective antitheses entails an important judgment about the order in which their two, opposing halves are placed. When Eleanor Roosevelt died, she was famous enough that the family required that her eulogist be eloquent; the speaker chosen was Adlai Stevenson. A sentence might have been cast, "She lit a candle when other people cursed the darkness"; but the more effective line *is* "When other people cursed the darkness, she lit a candle." As a general principle about antitheses, they usually read better or sound better as they end on the upbeat, emphasizing the positive. Yes, writers or speakers sometimes want to emphasize the negative. For all of the factors that made the age the "best of times," Dickens did want to assert that it also was the "worst of times." So whatever needs to be emphatic to readers or listeners should constitute the *second half* of the antithesis, for capitalizing on recency constitutes "the rule" governing the most effective use of the conformation.

Learning theory identifies and explains the behavioral laws about recency and primacy. Suppose that people are asked to recall a series of several two-digit numbers (such as 59, 34, 16, 92, and 78) that are quickly read aloud only once in random order. Two of those numbers have an advantage for memorability: the first one (*primacy*) and the last one (*recency*). Learning theorists' research also indicates that of those two, the last one is more likely remembered than the first one. So recency is more advantageous for emphasis. In any antithesis, the second half is the one read or heard more recently and thereby the position of emphasis; thus, its essential moral for an audience is placed *after* the "fulcrum."

In many instances of making antitheses, the objective is to phrase well some moral or maxim to guide audiences' behavior. This rhetorical endeavor is a typical task of speakers who are opinion leaders. In John Kennedy's most quoted line, what people should remember is to "ask what you can do for your country." Because it is in the second and hence more recent position, the moral is more emphatic.

RULE TO REMEMBER

Antitheses usually are more effective as they end on the upbeat. In lyrics for a popular song from the 1940s, you should "accentuate the positive." The better antithesis usually proceeds from negative to positive—*unless* the maker of the sentence purposefully wants to emphasize the negative.

As another case in point, President Ronald Reagan was called the Great Communicator. That title is not derived as much from his style in discourse, however, as from his ability to deliver lines effectively, with a well-modulated voice, physical poise, and superb eye contact. After all, we do not remember sentences from Ronald Reagan the way we do from Abraham Lincoln, Franklin Roosevelt, or John Kennedy. Part of the problem is that his antitheses do not follow "the rule" about accentuating the positive. For example, to make a moral about the best "government," Reagan said, "It is rather to make it work—work with us, not over us; to stand by our side, not ride our back." Those antitheses (more effectively) might end with "work with us" and "stand by our side," as in "not work over us but with us; not ride our back but stand by our side." Similarly, "The future is best decided by ballots, not bullets" might sound better as "The future is decided best not by bullets, but ballots." That format accentuates his recommendations about the future, the way Kennedy did with antitheses.[7]

To master antitheses, you must write them—and then rewrite them for (1) better balance, (2) brevity for easier recall, and (3) placement that emphasizes the positive by placing it in the second half of the antithesis (if that is what the line calls for in the way of deserved emphasis). Once drafted, any antithesis should be examined for what can be done to enhance its effectiveness. For instance, in his second inaugural address, Ronald Reagan said, "We have begun to increase the rewards for work, savings, and investment [and] reduce the increase in the cost and size of government and its interference in people's lives." The criterion about accentuate the positive applies here, and the two halves of the antithesis could be reversed to advantage. Moreover, by eliminating "the increase in" from "reduce the increase in the cost," the antithesis is sharper (because you do not have *increase* in both halves, to make them sound similar rather than sharply different). So to achieve more incisiveness and balance by having the same number of words on each side of the fulcrum, the line could be, "We have reduced the cost and size of government—and increased the rewards for work, savings, and investment." In this version, although the line is balanced in number of words on each side of the fulcrum, the second half—which expresses what people should do—*is* weightier and more significant (although a stylist might consider eliminating *one* of the second half's *three* elements—work, savings, and investment—to counterbalance exactly the *two* elements in the first half—cost and size).

 To achieve better-balanced antitheses, diagram sentences with see-saws to visualize how key

elements on either side of the fulcrum may create imbalance. Consider this line from General Douglas MacArthur: "The soldier above all other people prays for peace, for he must suffer and bear the deepest wounds and scars of war."

Soldier prays peace [for] he suffer and bear deepest wounds and scars of war

▲

This see-saw will tip to the right because of the extra elements on that side. Using the see-saw below, rewrite the antithesis for better balance.

▲

Balance is the necessary complement to terseness and "the rule" if a speaker desires antitheses conducive to memorability and quotability.

Now, practice making specific antitheses as they might be used in the pragmatic world of affairs, and perhaps the most realistic exercises appropriate now are drawn from the 1996 presidential campaign between Bill Clinton and Bob Dole. For the first exercise, recall that Senator Dole's acceptance address to the Republican Convention stated his desire to build a "bridge to the past." The rhetorical motivation was appropriate (as far as it went), for Dole wanted to emphasize his being the heroic veteran of World War II, in which he was severely wounded. He also wanted to portray himself as the product of the small-town, heartland America of earlier, virtuous times to which many people look back fondly. But in his acceptance address, President Clinton co–opted the line effectively by saying that he did not want to build any bridge to the past but a "bridge to the future." Dole could not use his line again in the campaign. Think about how Dole's assertion could have been more persuasive in the form of an antithesis about building upon the past for a better future. Using the see-saw below, start with *past* and *future*. See if you can make the antithesis for Dole that could not be co–opted by an opponent (hint: get rid of the word *bridge*).

Actually, your effective antithesis could have *future* on either side of the fulcrum. That is, in one format, to emphasize values of the "past," the sentence might assert that a successful "future," referred to on the left side of the fulcrum, comes about only by building on the *past* characterized on the right-hand side of the see-saw; but the sentence also could have *past* on the left-hand side to signify how it yields a desirable "future" articulated in the second half of the antithesis. This is the Kennedy way.

THE MOST POWERFUL ANTITHESIS

Any further reference to Kennedyesque antitheses should explain the particular uniqueness in this oft-quoted line, "Ask not what your country can do for you—ask what you can do for your country." *Learn this formula*: AB–BA; see it below as a see-saw:

A	B	B	A

Here is the "scheme" or plan for making this type of antithesis that is especially potent for quotability and memorability:

Ask not what your country can do for you—ask what you can do for your country.
| (A) | (B) | (B) | (A) |

Two key words from the first half, *country* and *you,* are reversed 180 degrees for appearance in the second half, and their reversed order has them say something directly opposite in meaning. Although the words themselves are not antonyms, or even opposites semantically, the effect of antithesis is obtained syntactically by reversing the order of their appearance. In classical rhetorical theory, this species of antithesis often was called *chiasmus.* From the Greek letter *Chi* , "X" symbolizes the "crossing pattern" entailed when making this conformation:

The AB–BA reversal is a powerful device for both impact and memorability. Kennedy used it beautifully, and so can you.

HELPFUL HINT *When drafting statements, be on the lookout for your use of any word which can be used as* both *a noun* and *a verb. Another line often quoted from John Kennedy is "Let us never negotiate out of fear, but let us never fear to negotiate." This is an AB–BA, based on "negotiate (A) out of fear (B)" and "fear (B) to negotiate (A)"; but in the first half,* fear *is a noun, whereas in the second half, it is a verb. A similar potential is operative in words that can be both nouns and adjectives. President Richard Nixon was fond of saying, "When the going (A) gets tough (B), the tough (B) get going (A)." In the first half,* tough *is an adjective, but in the second half, it is a noun (and* going *in the first half is a noun but a verb in the second half). If you find yourself making a sentence with one of those dual-use words, stop and consider whether it could be the basis of an AB–BA "reversal" antithesis.*

AB–BA reversal antitheses are difficult to create. But this sentence in discourse rewards communicators handsomely for their efforts. Think of how many successful advertising slogans capitalized upon them, such as "Pan Am flies (A) the world (B) the way the world (B) wants to fly (A)"; a cigarette commercial, "You can take Salem (A) out of the country (B) but you can't take the country (B) out of Salem (A)"; or a product that "won't add years (A) to your life (B) but life (B) to your years (A)." Even lines that are axiomatic enough for bumper stickers embody this conformation, such as "When guns are outlawed only outlaws will have guns."

An AB–BA reversal need not be absolutely symmetrical, however. That is, a word repeated and reversed for the second half can be slightly altered. In one campaign, I composed a billboard slogan for a candidate. Because he had two law degrees, had published in legal journals, and had taught in several law schools, I called him a "man of law." During a good year for "law and order" candidates who would be perceived as tough on criminals, I thought initially of having him "serve the law of man." But "law of man" suggested an anthropological phenomenon whereas "laws of men" suggested what people enact in legislative assemblies and other governing bodies. So I opted for "A man (A) of law (B) to serve the laws (B) of men (A)." Although "laws of men" is not an exact reversal of "man of law," it is close enough in form but different in content. Also, the antithesis is heightened by going from the singular in the first half to the plural in the second half. Although the language is now sexist and politically incorrect, the line was appropriate then. In his acceptance address to the 1968 Republican Convention, Richard Nixon changed a word from singular to plural in the second half to make his AB–BA reversal: "If we are to have respect (A) for law (B) in America we must have laws (B) that deserve respect (A)."

RULE TO REMEMBER

The second half of an AB–BA reversal *must* evoke a meaning in readers or listeners opposite or different from that in the first half. In form, a writer may be able to reverse the key elements 180 degrees, but the content for each combination can remain essentially the same. This is the case in "When the going (A) gets tough (B), the tough (B) going (A) can get you." "Tough going" and "going gets tough" are essentially similar meanings. Opposing meanings *are* juxtaposed, however, in "When the going (A) gets tough (B), the tough (B) get going (A)." The first version is a pseudoantithetical statement; the latter version is true antithesis.

To practice this specific conformation, write an AB–BA for either of the following scenarios. In his 1992 acceptance address, Bill Clinton described his childhood and the positive values he learned in the small town of Hope, Arkansas. He concluded his speech by saying, "I never left a place called Hope." In his 1996 acceptance address, he concluded by saying, "I still believe in a place called Hope." Hope can be both a noun and a verb! If you are a Democrat, dip your pen in whitewash and write an AB–BA for Clinton that capitalizes on the positive semantic connotation of the word and uses *hope* as either the A or the B in a *chiasmus*. If you are a Republican, however, you may dip your pen in acid and also write an AB–BA antithesis with *hope* as the *A* or the *B*.

To suggest the several options within speakers' capabilities for achieving eloquent style, look at the following sentence from the 1992 inaugural address of President Bill Clinton: "There is nothing wrong with America that cannot be cured by what is right with America." Yes, the sentence follows "the rule" and ends on the upbeat, but a more epigrammatic version would eliminate what in effect is the double negative and parallel repetition that make the halves sound alike:

"What is wrong with America can be cured by what is right."
After all, *right* deserves the most emphasis. But *right* has more
than one grammatical function, for *right* can be a noun, an
adjective, and a verb! Had Bill Clinton been inclined to project a persona more reminiscent of John Kennedy, he might
have cast some AB–BA antithesis evolving from juxtaposition
about "the right (A) of Americans (B) to make America (B)
right (A)."

SOME WARNINGS ABOUT ANTITHESES

For those who use AB–BA antitheses in oral discourse, a
caveat is in order. For all its potential memorability, this sentence can be difficult for listeners to process. After all, people
hear in rapid succession the *same* key words in each half of
the antithesis. The immediate reaction to the second half
might be something to the effect of "I just heard that." Then,
after a split second of a double take, the listener can resolve
the problem. But if too much psychological effort and time
are expended in processing the line (even for split seconds),
what follows the statement in that discourse might be
missed. So speakers are wise to give these antitheses special
care in delivery. Slow up and use the voice to help make sure
that listeners realize that the two halves *are* different.

Another warning is in order about AB–BA antitheses: they
can become complicated. Yes, the technically perfect AB–BA
antithesis has only four words, such as one that might be
uttered in Florida: "Alligators kill; kill alligators." The odds
are, however, that communicators need more than four
words to make meaningful statements in this format. But
these additional words should not take on semantic proportions of a C, D, E, F, or more. Without realizing it, speakers
can make a statement with an ABC–CBA format, for example,
or something even more complicated. In *The Art of Loving* (p.
41), Erich Fromm wrote, "Immature love (A) says: '*I love you*

(B) *because I need you* (C).' Mature love (D) says: *'I need you* (C) *because I love you* (B).'" Diagrammed for a see-saw, the statement looks like this:

| A | B | C | D | C | B |

For reading, at the reader's own pace, the line does not pose problems, for it can be reread to gain its import. To be understood easily during a public speaking event, however, a maxim may be too complicated because of the number of its terms. Incomprehensibility is not the case, though, in John Kennedy's most quoted AB–BA reversal, "Ask not what your country can do for you—ask what you can do for your country." The meaning is understood—instantly. And instant comprehension is vitally important for style in spoken discourse. If an audience does not understand the moral of the antithesis at the moment of its utterance, poof, it is gone!

The final caveat about AB–BA antitheses (or any sentence uttered by a speaker, for that matter) is also about complexity. Any antithesis should not require an additional sentence to explain its meaning. John Kennedy's famous line can be engraved on a monument, and no asterisk needs to be engraved after it, directing readers to a paragraph at the bottom of the monument that explains what the antithesis means. When drafting a manuscript for public speaking, any sentence that is at all muddy in meaning—or so long or complex that it is not meaningful immediately—should be discarded.

WHAT ANTITHESES SAY ABOUT THE SPEAKER

An important advantage of the AB–BA antithesis evolves from what its style projects about the prowess of people who utter the line. In discourse, readers or listeners are influenced by that "paramessage" whereby some factors, "although periph-

eral to the ideational content of the message, can materially
affect the overall impact upon the receiver." Those factors can
convey persuasively favorable "information about the source"
because "a discourse can provide *some degree of information
about the personality that created it.*" In particular, *"the language
in which the whole is expressed are forms of 'real' evidence* from
which inferences about the *competence, values, attitudes, etc."*
of the source may be drawn." The characteristics of a
speaker's *"vocabulary and diction . . .* are indicators of personality reflected in the discourse . . . *quite apart from the representa-
tional meaning of the message itself.*[8]

Classical rhetoricians used the word *urbanitas* to make the
point that anyone who makes an exceptionally well-crafted
AB–BA antithesis is no "country bumpkin," but rather an
urbane, sophisticated person adept with language. Thus, after
hearing "Let us never negotiate out of fear, but let us never
fear to negotiate," many people, at some level of consciousness, likely responded with a reaction such as "well said" or
"what an insightful way to say it" or "anyone who can compose that kind of line has to be wise and therefore worthy of
being followed."[9] The *chiasmus,* or AB–BA reversal antithesis,
often takes on the quality of a maxim or wise saying that
guides people's actions or attitudes, one that sagacious grand-
parents hand down lovingly to their grandchildren. This is
the case for "Some people live to eat, but others eat to live"
or "Some people hate to love, and others love to hate." For
erstwhile opinion leaders, *urbanitas* is a desirable attribute to
project as a communicator.

In the contemporary United States, we have ample examples of communication situations—from the pulpit to the presidential platform, from corporate boardrooms in Manhattan to
courtrooms in Los Angeles—wherein persuasiveness is derived
in substantial measure from admiration for someone's capabilities to articulate well what people want articulated well as their
fears or hopes or guidelines for living. As corroboration of the

power of John Kennedy's language, a college teacher of composition observed that students "enjoyed working with a piece of contemporary prose by a man of eminence, and they are pleased to discover so much to discuss about Mr. Kennedy's word choice, figurative language, phrase making, and variety of appeals."[10] The AB–BA antithesis surely is one of the most reliable ways to project a persuasive paramessage. Classical *chiasmus* can yield contemporary *urbanitas*!

SOME FINAL CONSIDERATIONS

Another species of antithesis should be in the repertoire of an able stylist. Novelty and hence noticeability of antitheses are derived from placing opposites in syntactical proximity. The absolute closest proximity occurs when two opposing words are in direct juxtaposition with no other words intervening, such as in John Kennedy's reference to a "peaceful revolution" (although a revolution, with its connotation of armed endeavor, seemingly means the absence of peace, it does make sense). When the two opposites directly juxtaposed are essentially antonyms, specifically, the "scheme" is known as *oxymoron*, such as the "bittersweets" of life, "healthful diseases," "profitable losses," "jumbo shrimp," or, one that some disparaging people deem appropriate, "military intelligence."

HELPFUL HINT *For* oxymoron, *the first of the two opposing words may determine the resultant meaning of the statement. In a "thunderous silence," for example, the reference is to a condition in which the total absence of sound is akin to the obtrusiveness of a loud stimulus such as thunder. This makes sense, whereas a "silent thunder" is nonsensical.*

Obviously, an *oxymoron*—or any antithesis, for that matter—should make sense, easily. People understand and appreciate quickly what it is like in line at a "slow fast food" eating place.

Still another mode of antithesis evolves from the apposition of homonyms (words that sound alike but have different meanings). Thus, "The parson *told* the sexton, and the sexton *tolled* the bell." *Told* and *tolled* sound alike but have different meanings and thereby create the effect of antithesis. The same is true in this line: "In thy youth learn a craft so that in old age you may live without craft." *Craft* has the same sound in both uses but differing meanings.

RULE TO REMEMBER

Do *not* use antitheses from apposing homonyms in *oral* discourse unless you are capable of emphasizing the difference in meaning with your voice. Listeners cannot perceive the different spellings and will be confused. In written discourse, readers can see the different spellings or have time to realize that homonymic words, although spelled the same, are different in their meanings.

Another caveat is warranted about these last two types of antitheses. Both *oxymoron* and apposing homonyms seem to suggest how clever the communicator is. If your objective is to create that impression, use them. For persuasive purposes of phrasing memorable morals and maxims, about significant issues and events, the better antitheses are those derived from antonyms or opposing words in close proximity as well as AB–BA reversals with the *urbanitas* that allows them to become not only sound bites on the evening news but also sagacious sayings to guide behavior.

KEEP ANTITHESES SHORT

No matter what their species, antitheses are ubiquitous in public discourse of successful persuaders because of their potential memorability as well as the favorable image projected for that writer or speaker. Nevertheless, this source of style is advantageous only if it incorporates another important principle: brevity. The longer and more complicated any antithesis is the less likely it is to be quotable. Keep antitheses short! This one rule is sufficiently important to merit further explanation. In the presidential campaign of 1964, the Democratic candidate was Lyndon Johnson; the Republican candidate was Barry Goldwater. Democrats tried to project an image of Lyndon Johnson as a prudent, cautious individual not likely to get us into war. Indeed, Johnson was advised to slow up his rate in delivery of speeches to help suggest that prudence and caution. Conversely, Barry Goldwater was portrayed as a "trigger-happy" individual whose rash decisions might cause war (he was the candidate who was understood to advocate Agent Orange to defoliate the jungles during the Vietnam War as well as to give commanders in the field the authority to use tactical, nuclear weapons). During this campaign, Democrats aired a television commercial showing a little girl walking peacefully through a field, pulling petals one by one off a flower, and counting "one, two, three, four . . . ." A "doomsday" voice then was interjected, uttering a countdown of "nine, eight, seven, six . . . ." The commercial then incorporated a montage switching to a scene of nuclear missiles being launched in what might be the onset of World War III. Many Americans believed that during that campaign, Barry Goldwater said, "Extremism in the defense of liberty is no vice," which seemed to prove the Democrats' point about him. Yes, Goldwater said that, but it was *one half* of this complex antithesis: "Extremism in the defense of liberty is no vice, and let me remind you also that moderation in the pursuit of justice is no virtue." If the line had been quoted and repeated by the media in its entirety, Barry Goldwater would not have appeared so extreme after all. But the line was too long and complicated, with too many polysyllabic words to be quoted in its entirety. Again, keep antitheses short!

When making antitheses, communicators sometimes inadvertently repeat words for parallelism in phrasing each of the two halves, as in "*he was* eager to arrive, but *he was* reluctant to depart." The second "he was," with its added length for the statement, is unnecessary and actually embodies two disadvantages. First, the opposites of "eager to arrive" and "reluctant to depart" are positioned farther apart syntactically because of the words repeated between them. The closer opposites are positioned to one another, the sharper and more prominent the antithesis. Second, repetition of the same words in each half of the antithesis makes the two parts seem more similar than dissimilar, for in oral discourse, the two halves thereby sound alike to appreciable extent. If two halves tend to sound alike, how can their meanings be opposites? Admittedly, the resultant paradox sometimes might be intended. Reconsider "It was the best of times, it was the worst of times." Parallelism of each half beginning with "it was the" projects similarity, but the antonyms of "best" and "worst" convey dissimilarity. The statement thereby is paradoxical, but perhaps Dickens wanted to pose that enigma at the outset of his tale. For most antitheses, however, repeating words or phrases for parallelism between the two halves will have more disadvantages than advantages. In the main, parallel repetition is incompatible with well-crafted antitheses.

To conclude about antitheses, do not be content with content. Strive for persuasive form, too. For more practice making antitheses, rewrite Abraham Lincoln's Gettysburg Address. Yes, improving on Lincoln's style truly is unnecessary; but to improve your proficiency with antitheses, try casting that speech as Ted Sorensen might have written it for John Kennedy. Immediately upon reading Lincoln's "new nation conceived in liberty," go for the antithesis! "New nation" might be contrasted with "old colonies" or "the Old World." "Liberty" has an opposite in "tyranny" or "oppression" (following "the rule," your antithesis most likely has "old colonies" and "oppression" to the left of the fulcrum and "new nation" and "liberty" to its right). To continue with such practice, consider how many words in the Gettysburg Address are nouns *and* verbs: *work, measure, place, ground, sense, note, long, resolve, cause, war* (as in "they war on their neighbors"), *power* ("fuel powers an engine"), and variants of *fought, honored,* and *advanced*—fight, honor, and advance. Pick two of these words and label them A and B on one side of a see-saw; then put them as B and A on the other side of the fulcrum to cast a *chiasmus* with *urbanitas*. Most likely, you could make two or three meaningful antitheses with other pairs of words from among these.

By exercising rhetorical sensitivity to consider and select from all the options available for a sentence, speakers are more likely to enhance the potential power of their words. Substance can be enhanced by style. Any sentence cast well as an antithesis is advantageous in discourse; the practices of successful speakers for centuries have demonstrated their ubiquity; and well-cast antitheses demonstrate conclusively the classical axiom that "a main difference between poet and poet, orator and orator, really does lie in the aptness with which they arrange their words."[11] Effective speakers know, though, that epigrammatic antitheses and other sources of eloquent style should summarize only correspondingly significant content that also projects credibility, as discussed in the next chapter.

NOTES

1. I cite the experimentation about those psycholinguistic constraints in "The Ubiquitous Antithesis: A Functional Source of Style in Political Discourse," *Style* 10 (Fall 1976): 426–441.

2. See P. C. Wason, "The Processing of Positive and Negative Information," *Quarterly Journal of Experimental Psychology* 11 (1959): 92, 102–

103, and Alexander Bain, *English Composition and Rhetoric*, enlarged ed., Part First (New York: Longmans, Green, 1890): 196–197.

3. Colin Cherry, *On Human Communication* (New York: Science Editions, 1961): 90, published initially in 1957 by the Massachusetts Institute of Technology; T. F. Karwoski and J. Schacter, "Psychological Studies in Semantics: III. Reaction Time for Similarity and Difference," *Journal of Social Psychology* 28 (1948): 104–105, 112.

4. Aristotle *Rhetoric* iii. 9.

5. For discussion of Richard Nixon's efforts in 1968 to imitate the antitheses of John Kennedy, see my essay coauthored with Robert V. Seltzer, "On Nixon's Kennedy Style," *Speaker and Gavel* 7 (January 1970): 41–43.

6. In the *Gainesville Sun* (19 April 1997): 2A.

7. I have discussed Ronald Reagan's shortcomings as a stylist in several essays. See "Ronald Reagan and the Presidential Imperative to Stylize: A – E = less than GC," *Speaker and Gavel* 20 (1982–83): 1–6; "The Impotent Style of Ronald Reagan: A – E = less–than GC *Rediviva,*" *Speaker and Gavel* 24 (1987): 53–59; and "Ronald Reagan," in *Fifty American Political Orators*, ed. Bernard Duffy and Halford Ryan (Westport, CT: Greenwood, 1986): 331–336.

8. Paul I. Rosenthal, "The Concept of the Paramessage in Persuasive Communication," *Quarterly Journal of Speech* 58 (February 1972): 15–17. Italics mine.

9. For further discussion of this functional effect of stylistic prowess and eloquence, see my earlier cited (see Note 1 in Chapter 1) "The Symbolic Substance of Style in Presidential Discourse" or "Alfred Thayer Mahan's Style on Sea Power: A Paramessage Conducing to *Ethos,*" *Speech Monographs* 42 (August 1975): 190–202, or Chapter 4 in my book, *History as Rhetoric: Style. Narrative, and Persuasion* (Columbia: University of South Carolina Press, 1995).

10. Burnham Carter, Jr., "President Kennedy's Inaugural Address," *College Composition and Communication* 14 (1963): 36–40. Italics mine.

11. Dionysius of Halicarnassus *On Literary Composition* 3.

3 CONTENT AND CREDIBILITY

Rationality is determined by the nature of persons as narrative beings—their inherent awareness of narrative probability, *what constitutes a coherent story, and their constant habit of testing* narrative fidelity, *whether the stories they experience ring true with the stories they know to be true in their lives.*

Walter Fisher, "The Narrative Paradigm"

The effectiveness of a communication is commonly assumed to depend to a considerable extent upon who delivers it.

Hovland, Janis, and Kelly, *Communication and Persuasion*

The primary purpose of this book is to explain nuances of word choice and word arrangement by which speakers bestow advantage upon their statements. However, wisdom dictates this very important reminder—to *any* speaker: Persuasive content and credibility are the absolutely necessary complements of effective style in discourse. An intimate relationship exists between form and content, style and substance, and ultimately, credibility. As Longinus observed, "sublime" style does not evolve from "paltry" subject matter but rather from materials reflecting a speaker's "grandeur of thought" and "lofty cast of mind."[1] Hence, speakers should appreciate some salient factors that undergird *what* they talk about in contradistinction to *how* they talk about their subjects.

FORMS OF SUPPORT

Speakers who deal with matters of substance must set forth ideas endowed with "rationality"—for information, persuasion, and inspiration—or combinations thereof. When those ideas are supported in effective ways, audiences come most fully to understand, to believe, to feel, or to act as the speaker intends. In the broadest terms, speakers are storytellers—as are all human beings; and in Walter Fisher's words, "rationality is determined by the nature of persons as narrative beings—their inherent awareness of *narrative probability,* what constitutes a coherent story, and their constant habit of testing *narrative fidelity,* whether the stories they experience ring true with the stories they know to be true in their lives."

> Any story, any rhetorical form of communication, not only says something about the world, it also implies an audience, persons who conceive of themselves in very specific ways. If a story denies a person's self-conception, it does not matter what it says about the world. . . . There are several reasons why this should be true. First, narration comes closer to capturing the experience of the world, and simultaneously appealing to the various senses, to reason and emotion, to intellect and imagination, and to fact and value. It does not presume intellectual contact only. Second, one does not have to be taught narrative probability and narrative fidelity; one culturally acquires them through a universal faculty and experience.[2]

For many rhetorical situations, "narrative probability and narrative fidelity" are achieved with the following verbal forms of support for speakers' assertions.

Examples

Examples are fundamental sources of persuasive content. As a specific instance of what the speaker is talking about, this form of support derives effective concreteness by employing proper nouns, that is, names of actual persons, places, or events. Moreover, examples are short, for they often are expressed in one sentence (or two or three at most), often introduced by "for instance" or "for example." Two speakers from the realm of military decision making exemplify the persuasiveness of well-chosen examples.

During the Cuban Missile Crisis in 1962, President Kennedy heard compelling arguments from his *ad hoc* Executive Committee ("Excom"), created to consider and recommend the response to Russian missiles being placed on launch pads in Cuba. Bellicose recommendations from the Joint Chiefs of Staff included "surgical" air strikes against the missile sites and an invasion of Cuba by American troops. One member of the Joint Chiefs was the voice of caution, however. General David M. Shoup, Commandant of the Marine Corps, conducted a briefing that utilized a potent example enhanced by a remarkable visual aid. On a transparent plastic overlay, he had drawn an outline of the island of Cuba. He then superimposed that outline over a map of the United States. To his audience's surprise, Cuba was not some small island in the Caribbean Sea but stretched nearly 800 miles from New York to Chicago. General Shoup then took another transparent overlay, with a small red dot, and placed it over the outline of Cuba. When asked what the dot represented, the marine said, "Tarawa," the tiny atoll in the Pacific where he had won the Medal of Honor during the war against Japan. He explained that "three days and eighteen thousand Marines" were needed to take what became known as "Terrible Tarawa," where inordinately high casualties (1,027 killed and 2,292 wounded) were suffered in the 76-hour fight for an island less than half the size of Central Park in New York City. President Kennedy once lauded Shoup for "lucid and incisive" statements that "as usual . . . went to the heart of the issue involved, and were praiseworthy for their direct and unequivocal manner of expression."[3] Any speakers today surely would hope to be so praised for their professional presentations.

Some examples require more than one sentence, however. In his speech that convinced the Joint Chiefs of Staff about Inchon as an amphibious landing site during the Korean War, General Douglas MacArthur offered a compelling specific instance of how audacity could lead to eminent success.

> As an example, the Marquis de Montcalm believed in 1759 that it was impossible for an armed force to scale the precipitous river banks south of the then walled city of Quebec, and therefore concentrated his formidable defenses along the more vulnerable banks north of the city. But General James Wolfe and a small force did indeed come up the St. Lawrence River and scale those heights. On the Plains of Abraham, Wolfe won a stunning victory that was made possible almost entirely by surprise. Thus he captured Quebec and in effect ended the French and Indian War. Like Montcalm, the North Koreans would regard an Inchon landing as impossible. Like Wolfe, I could take them by surprise.

A well-chosen example can become that "representative anecdote" so *"summational* in character" as to constitute a form of support *"wherein human relations grandly converge."*[4] John Kennedy's rhetorical sensitivity found a "summational" instance during his first televised presidential debate against Richard Nixon. To support his assertion that the United States was not doing enough for its people, Kennedy recounted his experience while campaigning during the primaries: "I saw cases in West Virginia, here in the United States, where children took home part of their school lunch in order to feed their families." Essentially, persuasive examples evolve from finding, as Longinus observed, "the most striking circumstances involved in whatever we are describing."[5]

Illustrations

Any example can become the basis of a more rhetorically potent form of verbal support: *illustration.* The best synonym for illustration is *story.* Numerous appraisals of discourse attest to the impress of well-told stories whose morals—whether stated explicitly or only inferred by audiences—become guidelines governing future attitudes and actions. One of the most successful speakers in American history was Russell H. Conwell, whose speech entitled "Acres of Diamonds" was delivered approximately 5,000 times beginning in 1870 and continuing for nearly half a century (he even presented it over the radio).[6] The speech takes its title from Conwell's opening illustration, a story told to him by an "old Arab guide" during a visit to the Middle East.

> The old guide told me that there once lived not far from the River Indus an ancient Persian by the name of Ali Hafed. He said that Ali Hafed owned a very large farm, that he had orchards, grainfields, and gardens; that he had money at interest, and was a wealthy and contented man. He was contented because he was wealthy, and wealthy because he was contented. One day there visited that old Persian farmer one of those ancient Buddhist priests, one of the wise men of the East. He sat down by the fire and told the old farmer how this world of ours was made. He said that this world was once a mere bank of fog, and that the Almighty thrust His finger into this bank of fog, and began slowly to move His finger around, increasing the speed until at last He whirled this bank of fog into a solid ball of fire. Then it went rolling through the universe, burning its way through other banks of fog, and condensed the moisture without, until it fell in floods of rain upon its hot surface, and cooled the outward crust. Then the internal fires bursting outward through the crust threw up the mountains and hills, the valleys, the plains and prairies of this wonderful world of

ours. If this internal molten mass came bursting out and cooled very quickly it became granite; less quickly copper, less quickly silver, less quickly gold, and, after gold, diamonds were made.

Said the old priest, "A diamond is a congealed drop of sunlight." Now that is literally scientifically true, that a diamond is an actual deposit of carbon from the sun. The old priest told Ali Hafed that if he had one diamond the size of his thumb he could purchase the country, and if he had a mine of diamonds he could place his children upon thrones through the influence of their great wealth.

Ali Hafed heard all about diamonds, how much they were worth, and went to his bed that night a poor man. He had not lost anything, but he was poor because he was discontented, and discontented because he feared he was poor. He said, "I want a mine of diamonds," and he lay awake all night.

Early in the morning he sought out the priest. I know by experience that a priest is very cross when awakened early in the morning, and when he shook that old priest out of his dreams, Ali Hafed said to him:

"Will you tell me where I can find diamonds?"

"Diamonds! What do you want with diamonds?" "Why, I wish to be immensely rich." "Well, then, go along and find them. That is all you have to do; go and find them, and then you have them." "But I don't know where to go." "Well, if you will find a river that runs through white sands, between high mountains, in those white sands you will always find diamonds." "I don't believe there is any such river." "Oh yes, there are plenty of them. All you have to do is to go and find them, and then you have them." Said Ali Hafed, "I will go."

So he sold his farm, collected his money, left his family in charge of a neighbor, and away he went in search of diamonds. He began his search, very properly to my mind, at the Mountains of the Moon. Afterward he came around into Palestine, then wandered on into Europe, and at last when his money was all spent and he was in rags, wretchedness, and poverty, he stood on the shore of that bay at Barcelona, in Spain, when a great tidal wave came rolling in between the pillars of Hercules, and the poor, afflicted, suffering, dying man could not resist the awful temptation to cast himself into that incoming tide, and he sank beneath its foaming crest, never to rise in this life again. . . .

The man who purchased Ali Hafed's farm one day led his camel into the garden to drink, and as that camel put its nose into the shallow water of that garden brook, Ali Hafed's successor noticed a curious flash of light from the white sands of the stream. He pulled out a black stone having an eye of light reflecting all the hues of the rainbow. He took the pebble into the house and put it on the mantel which covers the central fires, and forgot all about it. A few days later this same old priest came in to visit Ali Hafed's successor, the moment he opened that drawingroom door he saw that flash of light on the mantel, and he rushed up to it, and shouted: "Here is a diamond! Has Ali Hafed returned?" "Oh no, Ali Hafed has not returned, and that is not a diamond. That is nothing but a stone we found right out here in our own garden." "But," said the priest, "I tell you I know a diamond when I see it. I know positively that is a diamond." Then together they rushed out into that old garden and stirred up the white sands with their fingers, and lo! there came up other more beautiful and valuable gems than the first. "Thus," said the guide to me, and, friends it is historically true, "was discovered the diamond-mine of Golconda, the most magnificent diamond-mine in all the history of mankind, excelling the Kimberly itself. The Kohinoor, and the Orloff of the crown jewels of England and Russia, the largest on earth, came from that mine. . . . Had Ali Hafed remained at home and dug in his own cellar, or underneath his own wheat-fields, or in his own garden, instead of wretchedness, starvation, and death by suicide in a strange land, he would have had "acres of diamonds."

Conwell's illustration was rhetorically potent in an age when many Americans were restless. Because of intolerable working conditions, many laborers were forming unions to achieve redress; other Americans were heeding the advice "Go West, young man" in hopes of acquiring free land, gold, or other rewards. But the moral of Conwell's story for them—although unstated formally—was this: stay where you are; keep at your job (no matter how oppressive); for wealth is probably right there beneath your feet only waiting to be found.

Any example can become an illustration with (1) a compelling central character, (2) a chronology of events in which that character acts or reacts, and (3) sufficient detail that endows the narrative with believability. Although Conwell's story of "acres of diamonds" was longer, these three hallmarks of an effective illustration can be achieved in approximately 250 to 300 words. For persuasion, well-told stories often are about some person after whom audiences might model their behaviors. After all, people often "look to the discourse they are attending for cues that tell them how they are to view the world, even beyond the expressed concerns, the overt propositional sense, of the discourse." Although a story might suggest what people should *not* do (Ali Hafed's error in "Acres of Diamonds"), its characterization more likely portrays what Edwin Black calls the "beckoning archetype" or a "model of what the rhetor would have his real auditor become."[7] Chronology per se is important when depicting that persona because "story-telling is the most ubiquitous of human activities . . . it is the form of complex discourse that is earliest accessible to children and by which they are largely acculturated."[8] Specific detail is necessary for illustrations because, as Barbara Tuchman quotes Pooh-Bah in the Gilbert and Sullivan operetta, *The Mikado*, "corroborative detail" gives "artistic verisimilitude to an otherwise bald and unconvincing narrative."[9] To complement chronology essential for a story, detail lends it credibility.

Statistics

Speakers often must demonstrate that their examples and illustrations are not isolated instances of what happens in the world. For this demonstration, an appropriate verbal form of support is *statistics,* or numbers that typically show the relationship between the part and the whole. During his opening remarks in the first—and perhaps most crucial—1960 presidential debate on television, John Kennedy used statistical data to support his essential assertion that America was not "moving ahead."

> If a Negro baby is born—and this is true also of Puerto Ricans and Mexicans in some of our cities—he has about one-half as much chance to get through high school as a white baby. He has one-third as much chance to get through college as a white . . . student. He has about a third as much chance to be a professional man, about half as much chance to own a house. He has about uh—four times as much chance that he'll be out of work in his life as a white baby. I think we can do better.

In a speech that catapulted him to political prominence in 1964, Ronald Reagan's statistics supported his assertion that "no nation in history has ever survived a tax burden that reached a third of its national income."

> Today, 37 cents out of every dollar earned in this country is the tax collector's share, and yet our government continues to spend 17 million dollars a day more than the government takes in. We haven't balanced our budget 28 out of the last 34 years. We have raised our debt limit three times in the last 12 months, and now our

national debt is $1^1/_2$ times bigger than all the combined debts of all the nations of the world. We have 15 billion dollars in gold in our treasury—we don't own an ounce. Foreign dollars claims are 27.3 billion dollars, and we have just had announced that the dollar of 1939 will now purchase 45 cents in its total value.[10]

Statistics may be rounded off or specific; a speaker could say "nearly $1 million" or "$979,453." The former may be easier to comprehend quickly, but the latter may be more believable *because* of specificity. And prudent speakers probably will indicate the authoritative sources from which their statistics are derived.

Testimony

In many rhetorical situations, audiences should feel that assertions advanced by discourse are not those of merely the speaker alone but of other people, too. The form of support in this case is *testimony*. But testimony does not mean merely quotation from anyone else! Quotations become rhetorically potent as testimony only to the extent that their words are perceived by listeners as coming from someone whose opinion they respect. Thus, the rhetorical purpose of quotation is to suggest (by "name dropping") that the speaker is not alone in making his or her assertions.

During the 1952 presidential campaign, the Republican Party wanted to remove Richard Nixon as the vice-presidential candidate on the ticket with Dwight Eisenhower. The Republican concern was about a widely published charge that then Senator Nixon received and personally used money from a "secret" fund of $18,000 contributed by political supporters. On September 23, 1952, Nixon delivered a speech that told "my side of the story," and he utilized testimony from the "audit made by the Price, Waterhouse & Co. firm, and the legal opinion of Gibson, Dunn & Crutcher, lawyers in Los Angeles, the biggest law firm and incidentally one of the best ones in Los Angeles."

> It is our conclusion that Senator Nixon did not obtain any financial gain from the collection and disbursement of the fund by Dana Smith; that Senator Nixon did not violate any Federal or state law by reason of the operation of the fund, and that neither the portion of the fund paid by Dana Smith directly to third persons nor the portion paid to Senator Nixon to reimburse him for designated office expenses constituted income to the Senator which was either reportable or taxable as income under applicable tax laws. (Signed) Gibson, Dunn & Crutcher by Alma H. Conway.

Knowing that Americans had not heard of that law firm, Nixon enhanced its credibility, saying "the biggest . . . and incidentally one of the best." If quotations are particularly apt, but their sources are unknown to audiences, speakers should "introduce" the people being quoted for enhanced credibility.

Comparison

Comparison is talking about the unknown in terms of the known. When advocating his "Share the Wealth" program in 1934, Huey Long clarified persuasively his statistic that the United States was wrong "when the young children of this country are being reared into a sphere which is more owned by 12 men than it is by 120,000,000 people." He used this comparison in his famous radio address advocating "Every Man a King."

> Now, my friends, if you were off on an island where there were 100 lunches, you could not let one man eat up the hundred lunches, or take the hundred lunches

and not let anybody else eat any of them. If you did, there would not be anything else for the balance of the people to consume.

When addressing the 1988 Democratic convention, Ann Richards's opening asserted that "if you give us a chance," women "can perform" competently; for "after all, Ginger Rogers did everything that Fred Astaire did. She just did it backwards and in high heels." More recently, when speakers voice caution about American armed forces intervening in other parts of the word, from the Persian Gulf to Bosnia, one word often constitutes the basis of a persuasive comparison: *Vietnam.* From only that one word used about forthcoming armed intervention somewhere, listeners might recall what they knew already, that such endeavors can yield prolonged military involvement with many casualties, high cost, but negligible results for the United States.

The Ultimate "Soft Sell"

As another observation about persuasive discourse, speakers should understand that sometimes they are more effective when conclusions to be drawn from their supporting materials are *not* stated explicitly for listeners. This subtle mode of persuasion is known in the Aristotelian paradigm as an *enthymeme* (rendered from the classical Greek as "I recall" or "I remember"). A formal argument states its premises and conclusion explicitly as a syllogism:

All men are mortal	(major premise)
Socrates is a man	(minor premise)
Thus, Socrates is mortal	(conclusion)

In an enthymemic argument, however, a premise or the conclusion itself—or both—is omitted by the speaker, but the incomplete argument nevertheless is expressed in such a way as to cause listeners to "recall" or "remember" the unstated missing premise and arrive—*themselves*—at the speaker's unstated conclusion. An enthymemic argument was used during a civil rights demonstration in Memphis, Tennessee, when African-American sanitation workers marched down a main street carrying signs with these words printed on them:

I am a man.

Essentially, "I am a man" is a minor premise in an otherwise unstated syllogism. Upon seeing those words, many Americans might "recall" or "remember" the major premise they memorized as school children: "All men are created equal." Then, respondents might complete the worker's argument as, "Therefore, treat me as an equal." In some rhetorical situations, that "soft sell" is more potent than a "hard sell."

SOME REMINDERS ABOUT CONTENT

All of a speaker's forms of support should demonstrate that the attitudes or actions sought from audiences are consistent with, or fulfill, their basic needs as human beings. Persuasion or public speaking textbooks often list the "drives" that determine human behavior as well as people's learned ways, or "motives," for fulfilling those imperatives. One helpful guide to those possible bases of appeal is Abraham Maslow's *"hierarchy* of motives" including "(1) physiological needs, (i.e., food, water, sleep, etc.); (2) safety needs (i.e., stability, order, freedom from violence or disease, etc.); (3) belongingness needs (i.e., recognition, respect from others, self-respect, etc.); (5) self-actualization needs (i.e., genuine fulfillment, realization of potential, etc.)."[11] Whatever drive or motive is the most appropriate one to which a speaker might appeal is determined, of course, by an accurate assessment of what constitutes "fitting" discourse in a particular rhetorical situation.

In a book about the best words in their best orders, this final reminder is in order: communicators' uses of the various forms of support often are more effective when their total import is epitomized in well-crafted sentences, such as an antithesis. For instance, the wealth of specific details and testimony related to alleged improper behaviors by President Bill Clinton were epitomized with a potentially epigrammatic antithesis, "Americans don't expect an apostle in the White House. But they do expect an adult."[12]

ABOUT CREDIBILITY

The Greeks had a word for it: *ethos.* In their time-honored paradigm of rhetorical effectiveness, the perceived credible image, or ethos, of the speaker was deemed by Aristotle to be "the most potent of all the means to persuasion."[13] For credibility—and thereby persuasiveness—is conferred upon statements of those speakers accepted by audiences as people of knowledge or sagacity, high moral character, or no ulterior motive save the best interests of listeners. Now, the source of ethos known traditionally as knowledge or sagacity often is called the "competence" dimension of credibility, whereas good will and high moral character are subsumed under a "trustworthiness" dimension of a persuasive image, but this fact remains constant: "the effectiveness of a communication is commonly assumed to depend to a considerable extent upon who delivers it."[14]

Whether or not speakers truly possess attributes conducive to credibility sometimes is less instrumental for persuasion than the extent to which they are perceived to be so. In retrospect, Huey Long was not one worthy of national leadership, but to millions of his ardent followers during the early 1930s, no finer man walked the earth. So ethos or source credibility is the sine qua non of successful public discourse. Without this quality evinced effectively to audiences, whatever speakers say likely will not be persuasive. The last months of Lyndon Johnson's presidency were called the "credibility gap" because no matter what he said about the progress of the Vietnam War, too many Americans no longer trusted him. Phrased axiomatically, "What you are speaks so loudly I can't hear what you are saying." But when speakers do evince credibility, their potential for impress upon audiences increases. Put positively for speakers, your most important product is you.

What Aristotle recommended as the three dimensions of ethos are complemented by additional factors identified subsequently as sources of credibility in some situations: dynamism and similarity. In American culture, speakers who are perceived as moderately dynamic often attain an advantage from the robustness or physical activity they project. Because of the frontier and other adverse conditions that Americans historically overcame, physically dynamic speakers may inspire confidence from their listeners, who are products of this cultural heritage made manifest in our national folklore. In some rhetorical situations, speakers who demonstrate similarity with their audiences also may enhance their credibility. After all, listeners in many events confer credibility upon speakers perceived to resemble them in values.

At the outset, however, speakers should appreciate the difference between prior ethos, or what audiences know about them before they utter opening words, and "artistic" credibility created by the content, form, and delivery of speakers during their discourse. When speakers confront audiences with little in the way of a prior, favorable reputation, credibility must be created during the speech.

HELPFUL HINT *In many instances of public discourse, someone will introduce the speaker. Rather than leave so important a role as establishing prior ethos to a person who may be ill-prepared to help create that favorable image, speakers should have copies of an effective introduction already carefully prepared, one which specifies aspects of their background that can be stated in an introduction to help establish the credibility undergirding what the audience is about to hear.*

Of primary concern here, however, is what speakers say—and do—to enhance their credibility during discourse. Of the five dimensions of a credibility that might be evinced, perhaps only one is emphasized appropriately in some situations; in other instances, a combination of several aspects of ethos (if not all) are pertinent.

KNOWLEDGE OR COMPETENCE

Yes, much of the credibility that speakers project often is a function of a prior image of their knowledge or competence before they ever utter any words. During the presidential campaign of 1952, when the United States was mired in a seemingly unwinnable war in Korea, voters were receptive to that candidate consistently referred to in political advertising as "general." As the architect of D-Day and the defeat of Nazi Germany in World War II, General Dwight Eisenhower surely would know how to achieve victory in Korea. Indeed, his most effective campaign utterance may have been, "I shall go to Korea" (and presumably ascertain how the war might be won). In 1952, with that campaign promise, Eisenhower may have been "the closest thing in existence to an unbeatable candidate."[15]

Prior image can be reinforced effectively—and likely should be reinforced—during discourse, however. General

Douglas MacArthur had a reputation for military prowess, but he delivered an important speech wherein reinforcing that image was imperative. When addressing a Joint Meeting of Congress on April 19, 1951, MacArthur had just been relieved of his command of United Nations forces in Korea. President Harry Truman had fired MacArthur and recalled him to this country into retirement, but the general was invited to address Congress. To suggest that he was better informed than President Truman about how to wage war, MacArthur pointed out, "I know war as few other men now living know it." That assertion was buttressed effectively—and emotionally—during his concluding peroration about his "fifty-two years of military service."

In other rhetorical situations, speakers' use of detail and specificity evince the knowledge dimension of ethos. During the 1960 presidential campaign, John Kennedy was the youngest man ever to seek that office and therefore suspect in some people's minds as being too inexperienced. Although Richard Nixon was only four years older, he nevertheless emphasized the knowledge and experience he had acquired by being vice-president under Eisenhower for the previous eight years. Thus, Kennedy's opening remarks in the first—and perhaps most crucial—debate included that aforementioned array of specific statistical data that portrayed him as knowledgeable. He then was in a better position to counteract Nixon's charge about inexperience: "the Vice President and I came to the Congress together . . . 1946 . . . . I have been in the Congress for fourteen years. . . . I have met [sic] decisions over eight hundred times on matters which affect not only the domestic security of the United States, but as a member of the Senate Foreign Relations Committee." And perhaps Nixon inadvertently conferred credibility on Kennedy, when responding immediately to his challenger's opening indictment of the incumbent Republican administration, by saying "The things that Senator Kennedy has said many of us can agree with."[16]

The Nixon–Kennedy debates demonstrated that audience perceptions about speakers' competence can be altered during speeches. John Kennedy may have looked relatively young, but specificity of detailed materials he offered throughout all four TV debates helped create the impression that he was sufficiently knowledgeable to be president. And for a Catholic priest entering the fray of politics, Father Charles Coughlin's wealth of specific information suggested that he had not led a cloistered life but was well informed about current events when he spoke against the "Frankenstein of prohibition."

> Wine production of 1930 was 118,320,300 gallons, all containing twelve per cent of alcohol. For the five years, 1925 to 1930 . . . production of wine from California grapes was 678,320,030 gallons and . . . this wine contained 71,366,866 gallons of absolute alcohol which, in the equivalent of moonshine whiskey or brandy would be 142,733,272 gallons of one-hundred per cent proof. And all this in a so-called prohibition nation! . . . Statistics from 315 of our chief American cities as officially compiled by the police departments prove that there were twice as many arrests for drunkenness in 1929 as in 1919. Washington, our National Capital [had] . . . for the six years preceding prohibition 51,321 arrests for drunkenness on the public streets were made but in the six years of 1925 to 1930 this total leaped to 79,000 arrests.
>
> In 1928, the City of Philadelphia with less than 3,000,000 population registered 60,395 arrests for public drunkenness as compared with 55,642 convictions for drunkenness in England and Wales combined with a total population of 40,000,000. . . . There were 68,735 prisoners in State and Federal prisons and reformatories in 1910. But in the prohibition year of 1927 these same prisons housed 96,126 inmates. In England and Wales combined there were 9,508 prison-

ers in 1926, which is the last year of which I possess statistics.[17]

To access the widest range of specific information for his weekly broadcasts, Father Coughlin employed a large staff of researchers and editorial assistants, a factor that undoubtedly contributed to his exerting opinion leadership during the 1930s.

Potential danger exists when speakers attempt to project knowledge or competence, however. They may suggest an aura of "ivory tower" book learning too far removed from practical affairs to understand how things "really work." Although expertise founded upon academic credentials can conduce to credibility, Richard Hofstadter has described "anti-intellectualism in American life," whereby we often distrust people deemed too cerebral.[18] Such distrust may evolve when a speaker's vocabulary is "over the heads" of an audience. In the 1952 presidential campaign, the Democratic challenger to Dwight Eisenhower was Adlai Stevenson. Yes, some people placed his speeches "among the most distinguished oratorical efforts in United States political history." John Steinbeck said, "Until the convention I had never read nor heard a Stevenson word. And now we hurry through dinner to hear him on the radio or to see him on television. We fight over the morning paper with the 'full text.' And I can't remember ever reading a political speech with pleasure—sometimes with admiration, yes, but never with pleasure." Although a scholar lauded the "literacy" in Stevenson's acceptance address to the 1952 Democratic Convention, its vocabulary included "pretensions of individual acumen" or politicians' "imprecations," all of which portended "stylistic aloofness"; and as the campaign progressed, several observers sensed he "spoke over the heads of people." A political cartoon then showed Stevenson requesting that an aide use *Webster's Unabridged Dictionary* and, "Pick me ten big words that have four synonyms each. I must make a speech and I do not want to be understood."[19] In contradistinction to Eisenhower's positive image of practical expertise, Stevenson for many people projected a negative one epitomized by the sobriquet "egghead."

For Aristotle, the rhetorical counterpart of—or complement to—competence as derived from formal education or experience was the wisdom or sagacity stemming from age or simply thoughtfulness. Abraham Lincoln had little formal schooling, yet his image to this day is one of a sagacious leader. Lincoln's wisdom often was evinced by his sentences that exemplify sage advice: "A house divided against itself cannot stand"; "Truth is generally the best vindication against slander"; or "It is true that you may fool all the people some of the time; you can even fool some of the people all of the time; but you can't fool all of the people all the time."

HIGH MORAL CHARACTER

One word explains why Senator Edward ("Ted") Kennedy never could become president of the United States: *Chappaquiddick.* For all that he said and did to evince competence and goodwill, Mary Jo Kopechne's death during a questionable sequence of events forever precluded that possibility. The essential issue is that of high moral character. Yet this dimension of ethos sometimes is projected during discourse to overcome an audience's doubts about a speaker's virtue. With his "Checkers" speech on television in 1952, Richard Nixon alleviated doubts about his honesty. His use of testimony (described earlier) was effective, but his virtue also was evinced by portraying himself as a good husband and father to his children. The only gift he admitted to accepting was a black and white cocker spaniel puppy, which his daughter named Checkers. So he defiantly proclaimed, "You know, the kids love the dog and I just want to say this right now, that regardless of what they say about it, we're gonna keep it." One speech achieved an overall objective of demonstrating that the vice-presidential candidate was a trustworthy person who should be retained on the ticket with Dwight Eisenhower.

A Catholic priest was not likely suspected of lacking high moral character. Yet during the Great Depression, as he entered the fray of political issues, Father Coughlin's radio broadcasts typically emphasized his trustworthiness, such as when he spoke against prohibition:

> Ladies and gentlemen, I honestly wish that you will neither misinterpret what I am about to state nor take offense at the suggestion which seems to flow so naturally from the Gospel story to which we have listened. These thoughts come from the bottom of my heart. They bear a significance which at this moment is of paramount importance to everyone who pretends to be a Christian; who proclaims to be an American. . . . I ask you, therefore, to credit me with that amount of truthfulness which is devoid of both weak sentimentality and intentional exaggeration. . . . It is high time for us to put aside subterfuge and lying. . . . This is not a political issue of any nature whatsoever. It is God's issue, which is infinitely above politics.

Although Father Coughlin linked himself to virtuous values through *verbal* behaviors in radio addresses, speakers sometimes surround themselves with items *visually* suggestive of high moral character. What is the impression of a president who delivers a televised speech from the Oval Office and displays on the counter behind him a sculpted bust of Abraham Lincoln, "Honest Abe," and a framed photograph of his wife and children? During the presidential campaign of 1976, after the trauma of Watergate and Richard Nixon's resignation as president of the United States, any successful candidate would profit from projecting virtue and honesty. We learned that Jimmy Carter preached in his church in Plains, Georgia, and we saw campaign commercials that showed him at his farm there, dressed in denim jeans and work shirt, as a virtuous man of the soil. Jimmy Carter's potent campaign promise was "I will never lie to you." The honesty of that statement was underscored when he admitted, during an interview in *Playboy* magazine, that he had lusted, but only in his heart, after other women. Surely he was that open and truthful candidate needed after Watergate.

GOOD WILL

Speakers are more credible when perceived as motivated not by personal gain but only by the best interests of their listeners. Some statements are suspect because their speakers do not project good will. Used car salespeople often are seen as motivated solely by the ulterior motive of selling a car—and willing to say anything to do so. During the 1960 presidential campaign, a typically unflattering photograph of Richard Nixon was circulated with the caption "Would you buy a used car from this man?" (In 1964, an unflattering photograph of Democratic candidate Lyndon Johnson appeared with the caption "Would you buy a horse from this man?") Perhaps only a subtle distinction exists between the dimension of ethos known as good will and that of high moral character. Nevertheless, salient exemplars exist of what speakers say to demonstrate that they have the best interest of their listeners at heart.

After being relieved of command in Korea, General Douglas MacArthur easily might be perceived as having an ulterior motive of "getting even" by making President Truman look bad. To counteract—at the outset—any possibility of that impression working to his disadvantage, MacArthur began his address this way:

> I stand on this rostrum with a sense of deep humility
> and great pride—humility in the wake of those great
> American architects of our history who have stood
> here before me, pride in the reflection that this home
> of legislative debate represents human liberty in the
> purest form yet devised.
>
> Here are centered the hopes and aspirations and
> faith of the entire human race. I do not stand here as
> advocate for any partisan cause, for the issues are fun-
> damental and reach quite beyond the realm of partisan
> considerations. They must be resolved on the highest
> plane of national interest if our course is to prove
> sound and our future protected.
>
> I trust, therefore, that you will do me the justice of
> receiving that which I have to say as solely expressing
> the considered viewpoint of a fellow American.
>
> I address you with neither rancor nor bitterness in
> the fading twilight of life with but one purpose in
> mind: to serve my country.

Thus, after praising his listeners for their nobility, MacArthur
in turn reinforced his own good will by stating that he would
not engage in any "partisan cause," but rather speak "with neither rancor nor bitterness," but only "to serve my country."

In the "Checkers" speech, when he could have been perceived as only trying to save his political career, Richard Nixon
concluded by stating his less self-serving objective: "I would do
nothing that would harm the possibilities of Dwight Eisenhower to become President of the United States. . . . Regardless
of what happens I'm going to continue this fight. I'm going to
campaign up and down America until we drive the crooks and
Communists and those that defend them out of Washington.
And remember, folks, Eisenhower is a great man. . . . And a
vote for Eisenhower is a vote for what's good for America."
Similarly, when trying to persuade his radio audience that the
United States should not enter the World Court in 1935,
Father Coughlin suggested that his good will was so sincere

that he was willing to suffer because of it: "I take this stand knowing that, while I am expressing the thoughts and ideals, the hopes and the aspirations of the American people, I am on the losing side and I am subjecting myself to ridicule, to ignominy and perhaps to chastisement. But cost what it may, the American people have a right to know the unvarnished truth of facts."

The rhetorical potency of good will is illustrated in practical ways. The scene in a television commercial is a crowded restaurant; the noise level is high; patrons are conversing with one another; and the camera zooms in to one table where a person identifies his stockbroker's name and begins saying to his companion, "and my broker says." Thereupon everyone in the restaurant becomes quiet so they can *overhear* that conversation. For an overheard message obviously has no manipulative designs upon the eavesdropper. In an experimental study, an actor posing as a stockbroker sits next to someone on a commuter train, strikes up a conversation, and suggests during the conversation that the subject buy a certain stock. The person who heard the recommendation directly was then interviewed about his feelings toward that purchase. In the other experimental condition, two actors posing as stockbrokers seat themselves across the aisle from the person who will be the subject; they talk about that desirable stock purchase in voices loud enough to be overheard by the subject; and the subject subsequently is interviewed about his feelings toward that purchase. People who heard the sales pitch directed at them were less favorably disposed toward the purchase than individuals who *overheard* the sales pitch.

DYNAMISM

Americans tend to respond more favorably to speakers perceived as moderately dynamic (*moderately* is a significant adjective, for too much physical activity, particularly random movement, can suggest unfavorable hyperactivity). In addition to vocal and physical animation that accompanies delivery of an address, words uttered in speeches can suggest dynamism, as in John Kennedy's inaugural address:

> Let the word go forth from this time and place, to friend and foe alike, that the torch has been passed to a new generation of Americans—born in this century, tempered by war, disciplined by a hard and bitter peace, proud of our ancient heritage—and unwilling to witness or permit the slow undoing of those human rights to which this nation has always been committed, and to which we are committed today at home and around the world. Let every nation know, whether it wishes us well or ill, that we shall pay any price, bear any burden, meet any hardship, support any friend, oppose any foe to assure the survival and the success of liberty.

Someone espousing that arduous an endeavor surely has physical stamina. As we now know, Kennedy's physical robustness was more fiction than fact, for he had monumental health problems, which probably made it all the more imperative to display dynamism visually and to talk tough verbally. Franklin D. Roosevelt went to great lengths to hide his physical limitations, caused by polio: the steel braces on his legs were painted black to be less conspicuous against his black socks; he wore trousers too long to help hide those braces; and in those days, photographers honored a presidential request not to take pictures of his being lifted in and out of a car or of his being virtually carried to a position behind a lectern. Primarily from the vibrant voice they heard over the radio, however, Americans could infer that FDR was a physically dynamic person capable of the leadership required to alleviate the dire conditions of the Great Depression.

SIMILARITY

Speakers' attempts to project similarity range from the proverbial "I was born and raised on a farm" to a more current "I
was born and raised in a big city." In many rhetorical situations, advantage accrues from appearing similar to one's audience. In terms of the number of sentences projecting this
dimension of ethos, Richard Nixon's "Checkers" speech
exemplifies the appeal of similarity, for much of the speech
demonstrated how he was like the majority of voters:

> Our family was one of modest circumstances . . . .
>   I worked my way through college and to a great
> extent through law school. And then, in 1940, proba-
> bly the best thing that ever happened to me hap-
> pened, I married Pat—sitting over there. We had a
> rather difficult time after we were married, like so
> many of the young couples who may be listening to
> us . . . .
>   Let me say that my service record was not a partic-
> ularly unusual one. I went to the South Pacific. I guess
> I'm entitled to a couple of battle stars. I got a couple of
> letters of commendation but I was just out there when
> the bombs were falling . . . .
>   We live rather modestly. For four years we lived in
> an apartment in Park Fairfax, in Alexandria, Virginia.
> The rent was $80 a month. And we saved for the time
> that we could buy a house. . . .
>   We've got a house [now] in Washington which cost
> $41,000 and on which we owe $20,000. . . .
>   We have a house in Whittier, California, which
> cost $13,000 and on which we owe $10,000. . . .
>   What do we owe? Well, in addition to [the mort-
> gages] I owe $4,500 to the Riggs Bank in Washington,
> D.C. with interest at $4^1/_2$ per cent. . . .
>   That's what we have and that's what we owe. It
> isn't very much but Pat and I have the satisfaction that
> every dime that we've got is honestly ours. I should

say this—that Pat doesn't have a mink coat. But she
does have a respectable Republican cloth coat. And I
always tell her that she'd look good in anything.

The overwhelming success of this speech testifies to the
importance, during some occasions, of projecting similarity
to an audience.

Actually, several dimensions of a credible image may be
embodied within one precise rhetorical technique that is economical (in number of words needed) and appropriate for
some rhetorical situations: the two-sided presentation, or
both-sided argument. A thread of agreement among
researchers indicates that credibility for a communicator
evolves when negative or unfavorable material about a proposal is included with the positive or favorable material, particularly when audiences are opposed to the message or relatively well educated. After all, by acknowledging
counter-beliefs known or held by the audience, speakers can
be perceived as more fair and responsible in their treatments
of issues.[20] To apply this approach, speakers state overtly
those opposing arguments, and *some* credit is bestowed upon
audience members for those views. Thus, the speaker likely
begins by saying (in a hypothetical example), "I know that
many of you are very concerned about the high cost of
implementing my proposal, and I can appreciate that concern as well founded. I also know that many of you are reluctant to engage in this effort because of your objection to the
length of time necessary for it to accomplish its goals, and of
course your objection is motivated by the best of intentions."
The speaker's next word, of course, is *but*—followed by evidence and explanation of why audience members should
alter their previously opposing concerns. Again, a factor indi-
cating when the two-sided presentation or both-sided argument is appropriate is this: the more that people are informed

or educated, the greater the likelihood they have read or
heard opposing arguments to the speaker's position.

Even aspects of delivery—rate, pitch, volume, gesture, and
movement—are capable of projecting a paramessage that may
have positive—or negative—influence upon ethos. People
who listened to the Nixon–Kennedy debates on the radio
concluded that Nixon "won" them; television viewers
believed Kennedy "won." Pale, looking sickly (he had a tem-
perature that night), and perspiring freely, Nixon seemed ill-
at-ease in contrast to a tanned, confident-appearing Kennedy.
Even subtle mannerisms may conduce to credibility. During
his televised debates with the older (wiser?) Robert Dole, President Clinton displayed a tendency to pause, very briefly
before each of his statements, with hands close together and
index fingers touching each other at his chin, all suggestive
of thoughtful answers to the very serious questions being
asked. So whether in words or physical mannerisms or some
combination of both, speakers typically are more successful as
they complement content with effectively evinced ethos, the
"most potent of all the means of persuasion."

NOTES

1. Longinus, "On the Sublime," in *The Art of the Writer*, ed. Lane
Cooper (Ithaca, NY: Cornell University Press, 1952): 92.

2. Walter R. Fisher, "Narration as a Human Communication Paradigm: The Case of Public Moral Argument," *Communication Monographs*
51 (March 1984): 1–22.

3. I have discussed Shoup's rhetorical impact in "Barbara Tuchman, John Kennedy, and Why 'The Missiles of October' Did Not
Become *The Guns of August*," Chapter 7 in my *History as Rhetoric: Style,
Narrative, and Persuasion* (Columbia: University of South Carolina Press,
1995).

4. Kenneth Burke, *A Grammar of Motives* (New York: Prentice-Hall,
1954): 60, 324.

5. Longinus, 96.

6. A text of this speech appears, along with the speaker's autobio-
graphical account of it, in Russell H. Conwell, *Acres of Diamonds* (New

York: Harper and Brothers, 1915). Or see the text as reprinted in *American Forum: Speeches on Historic Issues, 1788–1900*, ed. Ernest J. Wrage and Barnet Baskerville (New York: Harper and Brothers, 1960): 263–275.

7. Edwin Black, "The Second Persona," *Quarterly Journal of Speech* 56 (April 1970): 112–113, 119.

8. Louis O. Mink, "Narrative Form as Cognitive Instrument," in *The Writing of History: Literary Form and Historical Understanding*, ed. Robert H. Canary and Henry Kozicki (Madison: University of Wisconsin Press, 1978): 133.

9. Barbara Tuchman, *Practicing History: Selected Essays* (New York: Alfred A. Knopf, 1981): 33.

10. The text of Reagan's "A Time for Choosing" is published in Halford Ross Ryan, *Contemporary American Public Discourse: A Collection of Speeches and Critical Essays*, 3rd ed. (Prospect Heights, IL: Waveland, 1992): 327–335.

11. See this overview in Herbert W. Simons, *Persuasion: Understanding, Practice, and Analysis* (Reading, MA: Addison-Wesley, 1976): 205; Maslow's early report of this hierarchy appeared in "A Dynamic Theory of Personality," *Psychological Review* 50: 370–396; or see his *Motivation and Personality* (New York: Harper and Row, 1954).

12. *Newsweek* (2 February 1998), 29.

13. Aristotle *Rhetoric* i. 2 (1356a).

14. Carl I. Hovland, Irving L. Janis, and Harold H. Kelley, *Communication and Persuasion* (New Haven: Yale University Press, 1953): 19–21ff.

15. Marcus Cunliffe, *The American Heritage History of the Presidency* (New York: American Heritage, 1968): 165.

16. For complete and accurate texts of the Nixon–Kennedy TV debates in 1960 see *The Great Debates: Background—Perspectives—Effects*, ed. Sidney Kraus (Bloomington: Indiana University Press, 1962): 348–430.

17. This statement as well as other quotations from the radio priest are from my book, *Father Charles E. Coughlin: Surrogate Spokesperson for the Disaffected* (Westport, CT: Greenwood, 1998).

18. Richard Hofstadter, *Anti-Intellectualism in American Life* (New York: Alfred Knopf, 1963).

19. I use this commentary in my essay, "The Ubiquitous Antithesis: A Functional Source of Style in Political Discourse," *Style 10* (Fall 1976): 426–441.

20. I cite much of that research in my essay, "The Symbolic Substance of Style in Presidential Discourse," *Style 16* (Winter 1982): 38–49.

4 METAPHOR

The Rhetorical Shorthand

[Metaphor] does not just express *the pertinence of certain cultural axioms to given social conditions, it* provides the semantic conditions through which *actors deal with that reality.*

J. Christopher Crocker,
"The Social Functions of Rhetorical Forms"

For people as "time binders" seeking to "bind past and future together in the present," metaphors can give a "futureness to the past and a pastness to the future that is fundamentally reassuring."

James W. Fernandez, "The Performance of Ritual Metaphors"

Illustrations, examples, and other forms of support require the use of many words. Similarly, establishing ethos or credibility can use many words, too. But one way of persuasive wording is very economical: one word or phrase that is a potent metaphor and thereby serves as a mode of rhetorical shorthand.

In 1946, the wartime prime minister of Great Britain, Winston Churchill, visited the United States. He was on a good-will speaking tour to thank Americans for helping to defeat Hitler's Nazi Germany as well as Japan. One of his speeches was delivered on March 5, 1946, at Westminster College in Fulton, Missouri (to honor its students killed in World War II, the college built a chapel that was a replica of one in London destroyed during an air raid; Churchill dedicated it). As the war ended in Europe, Soviet troops came from the east, regained lost territories of the USSR, drove German troops out of other conquered countries in central Europe, and ultimately took Berlin and occupied substantial portions of Germany. After landing on the coast of France in June 1944, American and British troops pushed into Germany from the west. The armies met in May 1945 along the Elbe River; Germany was defeated; World War II in Europe was over. But at their farthest line of advance, the Soviets created a boundary of barbed wire fences, minefields, sentry towers, and other fortifications—all backed up by tanks and the powerful Red Army—to seal off and protect its newly acquired sphere of influence. At Fulton, Churchill described the situation this way: "From Stettin on the Baltic Sea to Trieste on the Adriatic, an iron curtain has descended across the continent of Europe."

Literally, no curtain made of iron descended in Europe. Churchill took words that existed already and used them *non-literally* to describe something other than their usual referents. He made a memorable metaphor. "Iron Curtain" soon designated that boundary in Europe between communist east and democratic west. Not too long after its first utterance (and repetition in the mass media), Americans in Europe might enter a travel agency to buy a ticket for a tour to visit the Iron Curtain. Many of them expected to confront an edifice made of iron upon which they might bang their fists and elicit a clanging sound. So commonplace did the name become that *Webster's New World Dictionary*, for example, defines *iron curtain* as "the secrecy and censorship forming a

Soviet-made barrier around the Soviet Union and some other countries regarded as in its sphere." How a metaphor becomes literal is suggested by the following continuum:

fresh metaphor (first time used)	→	word metaphorical in origin (repeated successively)	→	literal word (in dictionaries)

To understand how Churchill's metaphor—or any metaphor—works effectively in public speaking or other modes of discourse, the purposeful nature of any act of communication must be reiterated: speakers' symbols should evoke meanings similar to those intended. Thus, speakers make metaphors *because* those words used nonliterally are more powerful than literal words.

Yes, much language on a day-to-day basis is metaphorical in origin. Many words that were fresh metaphors earlier became, through repetition, literal. When small, portable timepieces were invented to be worn on the body, words were needed to refer to the device and its component parts hitherto unnamed. After pondering the problem, an inventor might have coined a new word and called the product a "yof." With sufficient repetition, *yof* might have entered the vocabulary to signify the new item. But lexicon that existed already, such as *face, hands, watch,* and *wrist,* came to designate this new object and its components.

Researchers have compiled lists of the most commonly used words in the English language, and people communicate fairly effectively while relying upon a relatively few words in their vocabularies. But when some new situation arises—if a communicator's current vocabulary does not include appropriate choices or if a new word is not coined—lexical items already in use for other purposes can be applied in ways different from those customary. Inner-city ghetto language is rich in metaphor because educational deficiencies left many people there with limited vocabularies; but as their metaphors seemed apt, that language was adopted by still others wishing to be "cool." In the world of practical affairs, though, speakers will have other reasons for using metaphor—all of which conduce to attaining pragmatic objectives.

THE PSYCHOLOGY OF METAPHOR

Metaphor is *not* a literary device used only by writers of poetry or prose for refined readers or listeners. Rather, metaphors—or words metaphorical in origin—are omnipresent in daily language. For example, orientational metaphors predominate in "our physical and cultural experience," with "up" linked inextricably to happiness, health, life, high status, virtue, or power over others, whereas "down" characterizes utterances about sadness, sickness, death, or low status. And this usage originates in physical experience: "almost every movement we make involves a motor program that either changes our up–down orientation, maintains it, presupposes it, or takes it into account in some way. Our constant physical activity in the world, even when we sleep, makes an up-down orientation not merely relevant to our physical activity but centrally relevant."[1]

How metaphors evolve from literal words is viewed profitably from the perspective of psychological conditioning. With successive repetition and reinforcement, meanings become conditioned responses to words as stimuli. For example, the first time a child says "ma ma"—and mother hears it—positive reinforcement usually occurs in the form of a smile, embrace, kiss, or other approval, often accompanied by fulfillment of some need such as food. The child soon acquires a conditioned meaning for *ma ma* and then the word *mother.* When subsequently read or heard by the child, the word calls forth or evokes that conditioned response, or meaning, of what a mother is and does.

When a meaning evoked by a word as stimulus becomes the response conditioned to it by frequent usage, that word is literal. Yet literal words also might be used to signify something *other* than their customary referents, as in "Necessity is the *mother* of invention." People responding to that sentence for the first time will have their earlier conditioned response evoked by *mother* as a stimulus. But those respondents then must confront the discrepancy and comprehend that *mother* in this case does not refer to that person who, literally, is a source of life or primary caregiver but rather indicates that "necessity" performs the same essential tasks that a mother does. That new realization is an *un*conditioned response.

Because theirs are unconditioned responses, people reacting to metaphors experience a brief state of psychological imbalance called cognitive dissonance, which customarily causes motivation to restore a balanced state. For metaphors, that reduction takes the form of solving the problem of the discrepancy between the literal meaning conditioned to the word *mother* originally and its new meaning in a metaphorical sense. In a split second, that reader or listener must reach a mental conclusion, such as "Oh, I understand. Just as my mother gave birth to me and caused my existence as an entity so does some felt need or exigency (necessity) require similar means to solve that problem (invention)." Again, the *first* time such a meaning was evoked in a listener, it was that person's *unconditioned* response; for although it assimilated the conditioned response to the word *mother,* the new interpretation was unique for that respondent.[2]

Ideally, reduction of initial cognitive dissonance caused by any metaphor should take only a split second. If audiences take longer to resolve the discrepancy between conditioned responses to words and new interpretations desired by speakers, the reliability of the usage is deficient. That metaphor should be avoided. After all, people engaged in resolving a metaphor are not paying attention to the words following; and if cognitive dissonance is too difficult to reduce, audiences might "tune out" and not try to assimilate the message at all. But metaphor potentially is too potent to help enhance the power of discourse.

METAPHOR AND PERSUASIVE STYLE

In their first, fresh usage, all metaphors are deviations from the common idiom, discrepant with expectations, and thereby potentially novel—with an ensuing capability from their style to bestow emphasis upon a speaker's sentences. After all, people expect that the words they hear or read are used literally in ways that other members of the community use them. This does not mean, however, that metaphors per se are unexpected but rather that the specific word used metaphorically in its new way *is* discrepant with expectations—or else it would not be a metaphor. Therefore, effective metaphors do not evolve from uncommon words or phrases. Indeed, memorable metaphors often are made from mundane words. To deal cards anew in a poker game is a common occurrence and not particularly memorable, and the word signifying that act is familiar. But during the Great Depression, when Franklin Roosevelt characterized his forthcoming presidential administration as a "New Deal," he created wording that may hold a record for longevity in Americans' consciousness. And his metaphor, like all others, is a source of style.

One pragmatic reason to use metaphor is economy. In one word or short phrase of an apt metaphor, communicators may evoke essential meanings in far fewer words than if their statements were literal. In the eight words of "an iron curtain has descended across the continent," Winston Churchill communicated a condition in Europe that was described literally at the beginning of this chapter in more words. Or reconsider the six words in "necessity is the mother of invention" in contrast to these thirty-seven words: "just as my mother gave birth to me and caused my existence as an entity so does some felt need or exigency conduce to think and bring about the creation of some means to solve that problem." In this way, a metaphor is shorthand.

Speakers sometimes use metaphor primarily to inform listeners. To create knowledge when none existed previously, comparison is an effective technique, or talking about the unknown in terms of the known. Some metaphors achieve comparison effectively. At another university where I taught years ago, members of the football team were enrolled in special classes, including Speech 8A, "Public Speaking for Physical Education Majors." In that class, speeches to inform often explained "How to punt a football" or "How to put cleats on your shoes properly." But one student, who was a defensive lineman in football, also was a shot-putter for the track and field team. He spoke about "How to put a shot." Anticipating that his audience might not know what a shot was, he began, "A shot is a grapefruit, painted black, weighing 16 pounds." The metaphorical comparison helped his audience understand his subject (had he said, "A shot is *like* a grapefruit," the explicit comparison was simile). So in some communication situations, metaphors primarily inform.

But recall the fact that many metaphors are grounded in "physical and cultural experience." Generally, people appreciate that something made of iron is strong and impenetrable; a curtain descending means the end of the play when an audience no longer knows what occurs on the other side of the stage; and in eloquent combination, the resultant metaphor—when capitalizing upon these connotations of words—is an apt way of signifying persuasively what happened in Europe after World War II. And to consider this possibility is to move from the realm of words that inform to those with power to persuade.

From an anthropological perspective, long-term "social functions" of a metaphor reflect how well it aptly epitomizes a "truth of things" and a "prescription for action" answering the question "What shall we do about this?" For persuasion, that analogy created by a metaphor "does not just *express* the pertinence of certain cultural axioms to given social conditions, it *provides the semantic conditions through which* actors deal with that reality." Thus, for people as "time binders . . . framed between the remembered past and the imagined future with a need to fill the inchoate present with activity," metaphors can give a "futureness to the past and a pastness to the future that is fundamentally reassuring."[3] Words that are "reassuring" are persuasive.

Public speakers (or any communicators for that matter) should remember, however, that any metaphor is an *implicit* comparison or argument by analogy about the "thisness of that" or the "thatness of this." Simile, however, is an *explicit* comparison incorporating the word *like,* as in "He was like a rock" rather than the metaphorical "He was a rock."

HELPFUL HINT   *Any simile can be turned into a metaphor. Consider Douglas MacArthur's famous address at West Point. Lauding the cadet motto of "Duty, honor, country," he said, "Your guidepost stands out* like *a tenfold beacon in the night." He would have made a metaphor with but a slight adjustment: "Your guidepost* is *a tenfold beacon standing out in the night."*

By its very nature, the explicitness of simile (with its "like") *dictates* comparison. And speakers so explicit may suggest that they regard their audiences as intellectually deficient and unable to comprehend the comparison only implied by a metaphor. Conversely, the implicitness of metaphor arouses respondents' psychological involvement, which is consonant with the "psychodynamics of orality" described in the beginning of this book.

THE MODES OF METAPHOR

In the history of rhetorical theory, various forms of metaphorical expression were named with exotic and arcane terminology. Some of those forms are sufficiently important to be called "Master Tropes," as Kenneth Burke does. Their specific names are helpful to contemporary communicators because they designate precise ways of making metaphors.[4]

Synecdoche

The first mode of metaphorical process is *synecdoche*, whereby the prominent part of an object or being is used to signify its essence as a whole. As a Roman historian might have described the onset of a naval battle, "They saw a fleet of ten sails on the horizon." The most prominent and visible part of an early warship was its sail. Similarly, U.S. Marines were called "leathernecks" because their early uniforms included distinctive, high leather collars to ward off sword blows in hand-to-hand fighting aboard ships. An Army paratrooper will refer to an infantryman, who walks into battle, as a "leg" (as distinguished from someone who parachutes into battle). Indeed, many slang expressions for people are synecdochic, such as "redneck" to refer to Caucasian Americans whose social values reflect those of the rural South—wherein labor outdoors left people with a sunburned face demarcated at the neck from the pale torso covered by workshirts.

Some synecdoche becomes literal because of being particularly apt. On a U.S. Navy warship, an alarm bell is followed by the announcement, "All hands man your battle stations." A sailor is a "hand" because in earlier times, the prominent part of individuals who worked on ships (pulling ropes, tying knots, swabbing decks, or loading cannon) was their hands.

HELPFUL HINT   *As Aristotle once observed, makers of metaphors must have an eye for resemblance. The most reliable synecdoche may appeal to the sense of sight. That is, the metaphor evolves from naming the part that ordinarily catches our eyes first upon viewing the subject. Recall various metaphorical names children bestow upon other children, who have distinctive aspects of physical appearance: "four eyes" for a person with glasses; "metal mouth" for those wearing braces on their teeth. Political caricatures often portray individuals by exaggerating a physical feature, such as Ross Perot's ears or President Bill Clinton's nose.*

As Kenneth Burke astutely observes, sensory perception is "synecdochic in that the senses abstract certain qualities from some bundle of electro-chemical activities we call, say, a tree, and these qualities (such as size, shape, color, texture, weight, etc.) can be said 'truly to represent' a tree." So, the key to achieving a particularly apt synecdoche is to think of it as a word or phrase naming the part that is a *"representation"* of the whole because the "whole" as an entity may be too extensive to comprehend immediately from discourse.[5] For instance, during World War II, over a span of several days in June 1940, the British evacuated approximately 330,000 troops off an open beach at Dunkirk, France, under constant shelling, bombing, and strafing by the Germans. Prime Minister Winston Churchill called the event the British Empire's "finest hour." While comprehending a span of a week may be difficult, a part thereof—an hour—is more easily imagined.

Metonymy

Another species of metaphorical process is *metonymy*, whereby the tangible signifies the intangible. During the English Renaissance, a writer might want to communicate an abstract concept that people's accomplishments through intellect and language have greater influence than what they attain through force of arms in warfare. An apt metaphor was "The pen is mightier than the sword." When communicators seek economy as a stylistic goal, fewer words figuratively evoke a meaning requiring substantially more words literally. "Pen" is a tangible object representing intangible processes of the human mind; "sword" is a real item representing implements of war and their effects, perhaps known to people only in the abstract. Similarly, "beware the bottle" can constitute a warning about all the intangible effects of imbibing alcoholic beverages represented by their tangible container.

HELPFUL HINT *An effective way of making metonymy is to conceptualize a* touchable *object in use when an intangible quality is present. The nature of someone actively involved in the business world might be epitomized, for instance, by calling that person a "suit." While that apparel is not necessarily the most strikingly visible and synecdochic part of a person, clothing is touchable and characteristic of activity in which the individual is engaged.*

Kenneth Burke calls the metonymic process *"reduction"* of "some higher or more complex realm of being to the terms of a lower or less complex realm of being" capable of causing the same sense of *"consciousness"* as an item "so material that it can be reproduced, bought and sold."[6] Thus, contemporary "hip" talk used *metonymy* when a paycheck was referred to as "bread," whereby intangible buying power is epitomized by a real item that can be obtained therefrom.

Metonymy often capitalizes rhetorically upon connotations of words or phrases. In 1940 during the early part of World War II, German forces were conquering France with ease. Italian dictator Benito Mussolini decided to attack France and obtain some of the spoils of war before Hitler's army completed its task. France and Italy share a border along the Mediterranean Sea, where Mussolini's armed forces attacked. In a radio address to the American people, President Franklin Roosevelt denounced that aggression this way: "The hand that held the dagger has plunged it into the back of its neighbor." Literally, it is likely no Italian soldier stabbed a French soldier with a dagger (or bayonet). But *dagger* is a tangible object representing all weaponry that kills; and when stabbed into a person's back, *dagger* capitalizes connotatively on the treachery symbolized by that mode of onslaught.

Irony

While driving, you might hear a bang, followed by the car veering to one side and an ensuing thumping noise. After pulling to the side of the road and stopping, you walk around to the back of the car, see one of the tires flat, and say, "That's great." The situation was *not* great; you said the opposite of what you really felt; *great* was used nonliterally and thereby constituted a species of metaphor called irony. In oral discourse, the speaker's vocal quality of expression helps listeners know that the opposite is intended of what the words in irony signify literally. No such help is afforded to readers, however, who might understand the word literally and miss the point.

So irony is more reliable in evoking intended meanings only when speaking rather than writing. If spoken discourse likely will appear in print afterwards, however, the communicator might reconsider using a metaphor founded upon words that signify the opposite of what respondents expect them to mean.

If not irony, metonymy, or synecdoche, any other species of nonliteral figuration is simply a metaphor. And because metaphor is a source of style that can enhance the impress of discourse, guidelines undergirding its most potent use merit discussion.

PERSUASION FROM METAPHORICAL QUALIFIERS

Persuasion usually is the goal when using metaphor. In these instances, speakers (as well as writers) want their audiences not only to understand a message quickly as intended but also to be affected by the potential persuasive impact of the metaphor upon attitudes and actions. So words chosen for metaphors are selected primarily for their semantic connotations more so than for their denotative meanings. After all, many words as stimuli are capable of conducing to one of two basic behaviors: approach or avoidance. Connotative meanings of words used metaphorically can "serve as reinforcers effecting persuasion in receivers." Positive words "strengthen a response while negative evaluative words . . . inhibit the response. The strengthening of a positive response is termed approach behavior while the inhibiting of a positive response is avoidance behavior."[7] When following instructions to move a card with a word printed on it, subjects in an experiment found the task easier—in terms of speed and efficiency—to move the card with a word like *sweet* toward themselves than away, and easier to move a card with a word like *sour* away from rather than toward themselves.

Connotative or emotive meanings evoked by words often have greater potential to affect behavior than do their denotative or dictionary definitions. In 1896, the Democratic candidate for president, William Jennings Bryan, wanted Americans to reject (avoid) the gold standard upon which our currency was based and to use instead a silver standard upon which the printing of paper money would be predicated (America had more silver on reserve and thereby might print more paper money, which in turn might find its way more easily into the hands of the voters whom Bryan was trying to attract). So to denigrate the gold standard, Bryan said, "Thou shalt not press down upon the brow of labor this crown of thorns, thou shalt not crucify mankind upon a cross of gold." The metaphor was memorable and is linked forever with Bryan's name and platform in that campaign.

Persuaders also may desire to elicit approach behaviors, such as John Kennedy's presidential campaign theme in 1960. To make his administration accepted by voters (approached), Kennedy called it the "New Frontier." In a pivotal essay of 1893 entitled "The Significance of the Frontier in American History," Frederick Jackson Turner argued that the frontier had ended in 1890. Population density had attained levels whereby, with attendant ease of transportation, Americans no longer had as before a vast and dangerous wilderness to confront and conquer. But the appeal of our frontier persisted in our culture. We repressed unpleasant, literal facts of frontier life, such as log cabins with no indoor plumbing, central heating and cooling, microwave ovens, hot water on tap, and all those other comforts of contemporary life.

In the latter half of the twentieth century, though, the frontier is remembered fondly as the setting for gratifying challenge, adventure, and economic opportunity. When Kennedy sought the presidency, people clustered more than ever before in urban environments but had as their favorite television shows westerns such as "Wagon Train," "Have Gun, Will Travel," "The Rifleman," "Maverick," "Tales of Wells Fargo," "The Life and Legend of Wyatt Earp," and the highest-rated show from 1957 to 1961, "Gunsmoke." The connotation of "frontier" was more favorable than its denotative reality! And the frontier *still* appeals to Americans. A cursory view of television reveals advertising with cowboys lauding a wide variety of products, such as a steak sauce whose name they cannot pronounce correctly, and ads about vehicles having off-the-road capability, such as Ford "Broncos" or Dodge "Dakotas" that ford streams, climb rugged hills, and cross barren deserts—although most buyers are unlikely to use those vehicles in the ways depicted on television.[8]

For persuasive metaphor, whether to elicit approach or avoidance, the essential task is one of isolating first the *tenor* or essential meaning to be evoked about the subject being discussed. That tenor might be, as John Kennedy intended, a positive spirit of gratifying challenge, adventure, and opportunity, all to be approached; or the tenor might be, as William Jennings Bryan intended, avoidance of something anathema to Christians. Then, writers or speakers determine the specific word or phrase used metaphorically, whether *frontier* or "crucify mankind on a cross of gold," which is the *vehicle* by which that desired meaning will be evoked efficiently in readers or listeners.[9] But makers of metaphors must insure that their figurative uses of language, or vehicles, *do* evoke intended meanings. The speaker's insurance policy to ensure success evolves from what Michael Osborn and Douglas Ehninger call qualifiers.[10]

Contextual Qualifiers

Some literal words, either before or after the metaphor, direct readers or listeners correctly to the tenor to be communicated. Consider a classical Greek who would communicate economically the meaning (tenor) that Achilles was brave, strong, and formidable. That Greek might say, "Achilles was a lion," for a "lion" (vehicle) often is understood to be brave, strong, and formidable. But upon hearing or reading "Achilles was a lion," some people might visualize an animal stretched out in the sun, yawning, and flicking its tail at pestering flies. Another audience's influential meaning for *lion* might be that fostered by *Born Free*, a film about a lovable lioness cub raised by an English family in Africa. Those are *not* the meanings to be evoked when someone wants *lion* to communicate bravery, strength, and formidability. So the more advantageous sentence is "In battle, Achilles was a lion." The literal words *in battle* provide a *context* in which to interpret the metaphor. Because of that literal context, readers or listeners are less likely to think of a lion in a zoo or a cute lioness cub in a film (although "in battle" might follow "Achilles was a lion," its context functions better by coming first in the sentence). Similarly, the metaphorical "He was a hawk" is more meaningful instantly if preceded by a literal context, "In defense spending, he was a hawk."

To appreciate how rhetorical sensitivity may help create contextual qualifiers, recall the metaphor that President Bill Clinton hoped would symbolize his political agenda: "New Covenant." In the tradition of Franklin Roosevelt's "New Deal," John Kennedy's "New Frontier," and Ronald Reagan's tautological "New Beginning," Mr. Clinton wanted something "new." During the 1992 Democratic Convention, after his acceptance address outlined his agenda, Bill Clinton said, "I call this approach a New Covenant"—and he then repeated the metaphor 10 additional times! That extensive repetition reveals the hopes that Mr. Clinton had for the metaphor. But New Covenant did *not* become a catchphrase like New Deal or New Frontier.[11]

Generally, covenants denote agreements, vows, or compacts between people, such as a point in a legal document, if not the entire document itself. But *covenant* is familiar, too, for religious connotations. Often signifying a relationship entered into with a divine being, the word was widely used among seventeenth-century Puritans and subsequent New Englanders, particularly Calvinists and some members of the Congregational Church. Yes, that religious connotation might bestow an aura of moral virtue upon a candidate using that metaphor, for anyone espousing a covenant must be religious and therefore "good." But the metaphor has potential problems. Puritans acquired an image of intolerance, communicated persistently and vividly to Americans in novels, drama, and popular culture. Clinton's covenant would help groups enumerated in his speech: unemployed, underemployed, poorly educated, minorities, gays, unfortunate people addicted to drugs, welfare mothers, and women seeking their right to the "choice" of abortion. But these are peoples whom earlier intolerant Puritans would shun, and puritanical heirs among contemporary Americans might share that intolerance. With subtle stylistic emendation, the metaphor might have worked better. It would have been fresher if Clinton had eliminated the banal *new.* Instead, a contextual qualifier could help ensure that an intended meaning—one not associated with intolerant Puritans—would be evoked instead. Suppose Clinton had proposed a "covenant with compassion." In addition to salience derived from its alliteration, the metaphor with the literal contextual qualifier of "with compassion" likely would not evoke connotations linking *covenant* with intolerance of the past but would rather emphasize virtue in the present.

Practice Exercise

Write a sentence in which you characterize some person metaphorically as an animal, but use contextual qualifiers to emphasize the intended attributes of that animal. For instance, a wide range of responses might be forthcoming to "The executive was an elephant." But by adding literal words that specify the feature of the animal we should apprehend appreciatively, for example, "In his exercise of a prodigious memory, the executive was an elephant," the contextual qualifier makes the metaphor more meaningful.

Communal Qualifiers

A community of people—as a nation, region, or social subgroup—may acquire widespread shared meanings for certain words as stimuli. For example, the favorable meaning of *frontier* for Americans is not shared by Europeans, for whom the word signifies that place in the road where a crossing barrier painted in stripes must be lifted after one shows a passport to a uniformed official. That likely imagery for Europeans differs from that of adventure and opportunity known to Americans (although increased viewing of American western movies, with foreign languages dubbed in, may be altering Europeans' meaning for *frontier*).

Makers of effective metaphors are rhetorically sensitive to the repository of *connotative* meanings that a group might share about what should be approached or avoided, for only those words having communally shared connotations are likely to evoke emotional meanings that are persuasive. In American culture, a rattlesnake is far more than simply a denotative species of serpent. Rather, our communal meaning is one of a dangerous, particularly lethal reptile to be avoided or killed on sight. In 1941, several months before the United States entered World War II upon the bombing of Pearl Harbor, President Franklin Roosevelt as commander-in-chief of the armed forces ordered the United States Navy to fire upon and sink German submarines in the Atlantic Ocean. In his radio address justifying that decision, Roosevelt said, "These

Nazi raiders are the rattlesnakes of the Atlantic." Literally, a submarine is a combination of steel, diesel engines, fuel, torpedoes, and human crew. But Roosevelt labeled those German U-boats metaphorically as rattlesnakes, and all of the affective, negative impulses to avoid such entities—or destroy them on sight—was meaningful as justification for sinking them although we were not yet at war with Germany.

HELPFUL HINT *Some people may have unique meanings that differ from a group's shared meaning. These atypical responses to a word reflect an individual's private qualifiers. For instance, some herpetologists "milk" the fangs of rattlesnakes for venom, which in turn is used for medicinal purposes; their private conceptualization of a snake prevents the metaphor from evoking an avoidance response upon hearing it. Nevertheless, metaphors incorporating strong communal qualifiers should be persuasive for most people within that particular group.*

In the final analysis, communal metaphors offer *semantic conditions* through which people deal with reality. For instance, frontier experience yielded several metaphors to describe our subsequent warfare, thereby providing a "futureness to the past and a pastness to the future that is fundamentally reassuring." Long after the Native American menace to settlers ended on this continent, Americans described their enemies in twentieth-century wars as "savages" on the "warpath." Or, during World War II, American paratroopers fought an "Alamo" battle or were "pioneers" who "marched forth and planted the roots of settlement in the soil that was there for the taking"; during the Vietnam war, dangerous areas were called "Indian country," Vietnamese scouts were "Kit Carsons," and engaging in a particularly brave act was "pulling a John Wayne."[12] Faced with uncertainties about twentieth-century warfare, Americans could be reassured by powerful connotations consonant with approach behavior, by comprehending their endeavors as but extensions of our earlier national experiences—at which we always seemed successful.

Similar semantic conditions explain our communal preference for martial metaphors. When John Kennedy was elected to the presidency, World War II was still an event of monumental significance to Americans. Those who had not been in the armed forces were involved on the homefront, including children who helped the war effort in scrap metal collection drives, for instance. Kennedy's martial metaphors about a "beachhead" of cooperation or "now the trumpet summons us" were meaningful as they evoked positive feelings associated with that former great endeavor. His successor, Lyndon Johnson, accordingly declared a "war on poverty." Subsequently, President Bill Clinton's 1992 inaugural address lapsed easily into "we *march* to the music of our time, our *mission* is timeless"; we have *"mustered* the determination"; and "we have heard the *trumpets*. We have *changed the guard.*" These presidents seemed to follow the stylistic predilection of Franklin D. Roosevelt, whose first inaugural address articulated with martial metaphor both his intent "to *wage a war* against the emergency" as well as "the *lines of attack*" for Americans as a *"trained and loyal army."* After all, the language of war designates facets of the highly popular sport of football wherein quarterbacks throw "bombs," linebackers "blitz," linemen "fight it out in the trenches," and an "offense attacks a defense."

Even for nuclear war, American weaponry includes a missile named metaphorically after mythic, sharp-shooting riflemen from our earlier national experience: "Minuteman." For one way to make defense weaponry appreciated is to coin their "names metaphorically to make the unknown comprehensible and familiar." "Minuteman," specifically, prompts recall of "ways and weapons of the early frontier" and thereby a persuasive view of "missiles as muskets." (President Ronald Reagan in 1982 wanted to name the new MX missile "Peacemaker," after the Colt .45 revolver of frontier fame; but sensitive to a likelihood of political cartoons of him "with a six-shooter in my hand," he advocated "Peacekeeper" instead, which still is close enough to remind people of Samuel Colt's contribution to Americana).[13] Because of strong communal connotations, rhetorical discourse embodying frontier metaphors can be not only potent but also ominously so.

Reminder

What originally were fresh metaphors with communal qualifiers can be used so much that they become dead metaphors if not virtually literal language. For instance, most Americans understand the terminology of our "national pastime," baseball. Some of that language is used consistently as metaphors for other endeavors, as when a young man might say about some prospective girlfriend, "I couldn't get to first base with her; I really struck out." Such language now is virtually literal through its continued usage.

Well-chosen metaphors with communal qualifiers some-times are potent means of communication and persuasion *between* different cultural or national groups. John Kennedy's inaugural address was unique because it was the first one delivered to audiences in addition to Americans, such as "those new states whom we welcome to the ranks of the free," "our sister republics south of our border," and "those people in the huts and villages of half the globe struggling to break the bonds of mass misery." At one point, Kennedy said, "Remember that he who chooses to ride the back of the tiger winds up inside." That metaphor was not addressed to peoples in Africa or Central America or Cuba. Tigers are not emotionally meaningful animals in Cuba, Africa, or Central America. The tiger is indigenous only to Asia, where it signifies China (as the bear represents Russia; the lion, Great Britain; or the eagle, America). American fighter pilots in China, who volunteered to fly against the Japanese before Pearl Harbor, painted ferocious looking mouths with sharp teeth on the noses of their P-40 aircraft. They first called themselves Flying Tiger Sharks, after the creature that maritime Japanese greatly feared, but someone pointed out that the animal symbolizing China was the tiger, so their name was changed to Flying Tigers. Thus, in 1961, to new nations in Southeast Asia, Kennedy's metaphor was meaningful: China may offer you military aid and advisors; but if you allow a few of them in, more will follow and soon take over your country from within. So do not accept military aid and "ride the back" of China.

Practice Exercise

Make a fresh metaphor, embodying a communal qualifier from a sport, to characterize the essential nature of some particular business or governmental activity, such as "This advertising agency made a slam dunk when securing the account of that major corporation, and we will protect our new lead with a tenacious full court press." If you make this metaphor with terminology from a sport with which your audience is very familiar, a contextual qualifier likely is unnecessary.

Archetypal Qualifiers

The significantly more powerful connotations that are particularly apt for metaphors are those that endow a word or phrase with archetypal qualifiers. That is, regardless of the social or national group for whom it is intended, the metaphor likely is persuasive because its connotation is universally understood, across cultures. As Michael Osborn observes, some metaphors "place figurative value judgments upon subjects" so "immune to changes wrought by time" that "meanings come across the barriers raised by time and cultural change." Moreover, these "archetypal metaphors are grounded in prominent features of experience, in objects, actions, or conditions which are inescapably salient in human consciousness" and thereby embody "basic human motivations."[14]

Abraham Lincoln's Gettysburg Address used archetypal life-cycle metaphors whereby the American nation was "conceived" in liberty and had a new "birth" of freedom but nevertheless was in danger that it might "perish." Approximately nine months before July 4, 1776, George Washington might have been on a trip to Philadelphia to raise money for a new Continental Army. Perhaps he stopped at Betsy Ross's house to inquire about her progress in designing and sewing a flag for the emerging independent country. On a cold, rainy evening, he might have been invited in to warm himself by the fire and have a few hot rum toddies with Betsy, who was home alone that night and was attracted to her visitor. Yes, human beings literally are conceived, are born, live, and then perish. Although George Washington may have been "the father of his country" (in more ways than one), no nation was "conceived" that night so that it later might be born. To describe a nation that way is to be figurative; but Lincoln's Gettysburg Address thereby embodied archetypal qualifiers because everyone understands the import of those concepts and responds in characteristically common ways.

Practice Exercise

Cast a sentence in which you use an archetypal, life-cycle metaphor to epitomize the role or progress of a governmental agency in addressing its task, such as "NASA has progressed from the adolescence of its early probes into space to the adulthood of interplanetary exploration." As a way of facilitating your use of this species of archetypal qualifier, make a list of still other phases in the cycle of life, for example, infancy, childhood, old age, or perhaps senility, all of which might be used metaphorically.

To illustrate further how archetypal qualifiers operate in metaphor, virtually any group or culture likely regards a rock as solid and secure. So an insurance company suggests its stability by referring to itself, by word and picture, as "the rock." Regardless of education or experience, people can respond positively with an evoked meaning of solidity or stability as a characteristic of that company. For these people, *rock* as shorthand has influential archetypal qualifiers because of connotations evoked by that single word used figuratively. Some of those people, however, may belong to a communal entity that is sufficiently well informed about history to know that the specific "rock" depicted visually in the television commercial is that of Gibraltar, the impregnable British fortress guarding the entrance to the Mediterranean Sea from the Atlantic Ocean. For these people, *rock* also has an influential communal qualifier.

An exceptionally effective source of archetypal metaphor is founded upon light and dark. Across cultures, something that is a source of light is good; conversely, darkness is bad. As Michael Osborn observes about these archetypal metaphors, "the nature of these motives and the rationale for their attachment to light and darkness are immediately apparent."

Light (and the day) relates to the fundamental struggle
for survival and development. Light is a condition for
sight, the most essential of man's sensory attachments
to the world about him. With light and sight one is
informed of his environment, can escape its dangers,
can take advantage of its rewards, and can even exert
some influence over its nature. Light also means the
warmth and engendering power of the sun, which
enable both directly and indirectly man's physical
development.

In utter contrast is darkness (and the night), bringing
fear of the unknown, discouraging sight, making one
ignorant of his environment—vulnerable to its dangers
and blind to its rewards. One is reduced to a helpless
state, no longer able to control the world about him.
Finally, darkness is cold, suggesting stagnation and
thoughts of the grave.[15]

The pervasive—and persuasive—negative connotation of
darkness has led to many metaphors becoming dead
metaphors, if not virtually literal references to unpleasant or
harmful situations. For an act violating governmental or business norms, for instance, you are put not on a "white list"
but on a "black list" (Hollywood actors and directors who
allegedly were Communist sympathizers were "blacklisted"
and not allowed to work again in the industry). Similarly,
when the secret vote of a college fraternity disallowed your
membership, you were not "whiteballed" but "blackballed"
(and how many people upon finding themselves in a difficult
situation refer to themselves as "behind the eightball," which
is black).

The appeal of light and avoidance of darkness likely are
common in humans. In caveman days, darkness was a place of
unknown terror, whereas warmth and light from fires sus-
tained life (recall how often you have found yourself staring,

virtually mesmerized, at burning logs in a fireplace or a bonfire at the beach). So to suggest, in highly affective ways, that some course of action is desirable and worthy of being approached, describe it with metaphors about light, such as John Kennedy's inaugural address reference to "the glow of that endeavor" or "now the torch is passed." Similarly, Martin Luther King, Jr., called the Emancipation Proclamation "a great beacon light of hope to millions of Negro slaves" and called upon Americans to follow "the sunlit path of racial justice"; and President Bill Clinton's inaugural address in 1992 noted that although Americans had been "raised in the shadows of the Cold War," they now were "warmed by the sunshine of freedom."

Conversely, to suggest that something is bad, undesirable, sad, or worthy of being avoided, describe it with dark metaphors, such as Kennedy's reference to the "dark powers of destruction" brought about by science or the "long, twilight struggle" of the Cold War. To refer obliquely to his impending death from old age, Douglas MacArthur's speech at West Point reminded cadets that "the shadows are lengthening for me. The twilight is here." And speakers might combine the two, apposing connotations of light and dark metaphors into antitheses, such as that about Eleanor Roosevelt: "When other people cursed the darkness, she lit a candle." When using archetypal metaphors, speakers capitalize on the likelihood that people as "time binders" seek activity that will "bind past and future together in the present"; and metaphors with those strong archetypal qualifiers residing *within* the figurative word as vehicle give a "futureness to the past and a pastness to the future that is fundamentally reassuring."

Metaphors with archetypal qualifiers are so potent that speakers and other communicators will profit from understanding their several reliable sources. The following list, although a partial one, suggests figurations that are applicable in a wide range of persuasive discourse:

High and Low

Recall those *"orientational metaphors"* whereby *up* is linked inextricably to happiness, health, life, high status, or virtue, and *down* characterizes utterances about sadness, sickness, death, low status. Martin Luther King, Jr., used one to contrast a "sunlit path of racial justice" with the "dark and desolate valley of segregation"; another said, "now is the time to lift our nation from the quicksand of racial injustice to the solid rock of brotherhood" (of course *rock, dark,* and *sunlit* are archetypal metaphors, too). Archetypal notions of high and low often complement those of light and dark for particularly potent metaphors, such as that in the 23rd Psalm referring to "the valley of the shadow of death."

Change of Seasons

The change of seasons is inexorable, and metaphors are potentially affective when they suggest that the cold of winter (negative) will be replaced by the warmth of spring and summer (positive). In his 1992 inaugural address, President Bill Clinton asserted that by their votes for a Democratic candidate, "Americans have *forced the spring,*" and "now, we must do the work the *season* demands." Moreover, "our renewal" thereby entails for Americans a *"season of service."* In so doing, he used metaphor similar to that in Franklin Roosevelt's first inaugural address, which described the dire economic conditions of the Great Depression as "the means of exchange are *frozen* in the currents of trade; the *withered leaves* of industrial enterprise lie on every side."

The Sea

Oceans are intrinsically appealing and atavistically so. Many people buy properties whose monetary value is increased significantly because of being immediately adjacent to bodies of water or having views of the water. Indeed, "across many cultures, the sea as symbol touches off those depth responses" and "emotions which can lend . . . a special urgency to rhetoric."[16] As Martin Luther King, Jr., said in his "I Have a Dream" speech, "The Negro lives on a lonely island of poverty in the midst of a vast ocean of material prosperity" (which also is an antithesis).

Diseases

Cancer has powerful connotations capable of inducing avoidance behavior. In a dictionary definition, cancer is "any of various neoplasms that manifest invasiveness and a tendency to metastasize to new sites" and "the pathological condition characterized by such growth." But that denotative meaning is not as frightening as the connotation of *cancer.* When told they have cancer, many people assume only the most dire consequences—suffering and certain death. Despite advances in medical technologies for treating the disease, doctors have a difficult time dispelling those fears because of the powerful, negative connotations of the word. Cancer *is* a condition to avoid if at all possible, so if some social or political condition also is to be avoided, call it a "cancer"; it will be deemed pernicious or likely to cause suffering or death. Americans often heard or read metaphors about crime or drugs or Communism as a "cancer." The word *AIDS* is a similar metaphorical source of avoidance behavior, such as when a speaker might refer to insider trading as the AIDS of Wall Street.

Snakes

In the spring of 1941, Franklin Roosevelt's depiction of German submarines as rattlesnakes embodied a communal qualifier because that particular serpent is indigenous only to North America. Nevertheless, *snake* has a negative connotation that extends well beyond North America to be pervasive in other cultures as well, thereby assuming archetypal proportions. In the doctrine of Christianity, the temptation of Eve in the Garden of Eden was initiated and abetted by a serpent, "more subtle than any beast of the field that the Lord God had made" (Gen. 3). In Greek mythology, Medusa's horrific image as a goddess was emphasized by the fact that her hair was composed of snakes. So some person who committed or will commit an act of treachery from a hidden position is a "snake in the grass."

Natural Phenomena of Major Consequence

People lapse easily into metaphors originating in a phenomenon of nature with serious, if not dire, consequences. We speak easily of a *"torrent* of angry words" coming from someone; people were beset by an *"avalanche* of economic problems"; an *"earthquake* struck the financial world"; the agency was overwhelmed by a *"flood* of paperwork that *inundated* the office"; the hospital was *"swamped by a tidal wave"* of epidemic cases; or the armored division attacked the enemy position with *"lightning* speed" (German mechanized forces so successful in the opening months of World War II were engaged in a mode of operations called "Blitzkrieg," that is, lightning war).

Some final advice about metaphor: Effective figurations appeal to sensory experiences—what people see, hear, feel, smell, or taste. Of all the senses to which metaphors might appeal, however, those of sight and feel (tactile sensation) are the most reliable. The pivotal factor accounting for this likelihood is the *duration* with which various sensory experiences are present to us. Smell or tastes are present to people for comparatively short times, perhaps only seconds. Some sounds are present for longer durations of time, and a tactile sensation of something we feel may be as long in duration as we are awake, as is the case of someone wearing shoes that are too tight all day long. But what we *see* potentially is the sensory experience of the longest duration, present to us for as long as we are awake on a given day and perhaps for successive days or longer. Therefore, metaphors evoking meanings about something we have seen are potentially more reliable than others.

To conclude, metaphor does "not just *express* the pertinence of certain cultural axioms to given social conditions, it *provides the semantic conditions through which* actors deal with that reality." Semantic conditions can and do affect physical action. For example, research in physiological psychology suggests that physically impaired people who ostensibly can no longer perform specific motor functions are able to do so when given verbal commands to perform *other*, strongly associated motor functions. In the terminology of physiological psychology, the improved walk is the result of "self-initiated *re*afferent recruitment of allied reflexes." Patients who cannot rise voluntarily from a sitting position nevertheless do so when told to catch the ball thrown to them. A Parkinson's victim who is "frozen" and does not "walk" voluntarily nevertheless does so when told to "step over the wad of paper on the floor." (Some victims of the disease carry wads of paper to place on the floor in front of them to trigger indirectly the formerly impossible motor activity of walking.)[17] So figurative language through metaphor indeed can provide people with a persuasive "futureness to the past and a pastness to the future that is fundamentally reassuring."

NOTES

1. George Lakoff and Mark Johnson, *Metaphors We Live By* (Chicago: University of Chicago Press, 1980): 1, 14–19, 56–57.

2. For discussion of metaphor evoking conditioned and unconditioned responses, as well as the attendant novelty therefrom, see William Jordan, "Toward a Psychological Theory of Metaphor," *Western Journal of Speech Communication* 35 (Summer 1971): 169–175.

3. J. Christopher Crocker, "The Social Functions of Rhetorical Forms" and James W. Fernandez, "The Performance of Ritual Metaphor," both in *The Social Use of Metaphor: Essays on the Anthropology of Rhetoric*, ed. J. David Sapir and J. Christopher Crocker (Philadelphia: University of Pennsylvania Press, 1977): 37–39, 46–47, and 118.

4. Kenneth Burke, *A Grammar of Motives* (New York: Prentice-Hall, 1954): 503–517.

5. Burke, 508 and 503.

6. Burke, 503–509.

7. William J. Jordan, "A Reinforcement Model of Metaphor," *Speech Monographs* 39 (August 1972): 223–226.

8. I have discussed the appeal of the frontier in contemporary American life in *History as Rhetoric: Style, Narrative, and Persuasion* (Columbia: University of South Carolina Press, 1995).

9. For further discussion of metaphor as the interaction of tenor and vehicle, see Michael Osborn and Douglas Ehninger, "The Metaphor in Public Address," *Speech Monographs* 29 (August 1962): 223–234 as well as William Jordan and W. Clifton Adams, "I. A. Richards' Concept of Tenor-Vehicle Interaction," *Central States Speech Journal* 27 (Summer 1976): 136–143.

10. Osborn and Ehninger, *ibid.*

11. For a more complete analysis of Clinton's predilections for syntax and lexicon, see Ronald H. Carpenter, "The Stylistic Persona of Bill Clinton: From Arkansas and Aristotelian Attica," in *Bill Clinton on Stump, State, and Stage: The Rhetorical Road to the White House*, ed. Stephen A. Smith (Fayetteville: University of Arkansas Press, 1994): 101–132.

12. For a comprehensive survey of the development of this particular analogy, see Ronald H. Carpenter, "America's Tragic Metaphor: Our Twentieth-Century Combatants as Frontiersmen," *Quarterly Journal of Speech* 76 (February 1990): 1–22, as well as Chapter 8 of my book, *History as Rhetoric, ibid.*

13. See Charles Kauffman, "Names and Weapons," *Communication Monographs* 56 (September 1989): 277–281.

14. Michael Osborn, "Archetypal Metaphor in Rhetoric: The Light–Dark Family," *Quarterly Journal of Speech* 53 (April 1967): 116, 120–121.

15. Osborn, "Archetypal Metaphor," 117.

16. Michael Osborn, "The Evolution of the Archetypal Sea in Rhetoric and Poetic," *Quarterly Journal of Speech* 63 (December 1977): 347–363.

17. For these insights and terminology, I am deeply indebted to Philip Teitelbaum, Graduate Research Professor of Psychology, University of Florida.

5 REPEATING AND OMITTING—POINT AND COUNTERPOINT

The repetition *of a stimulus helps in several ways to evoke action.*

Boring, Langfeld, and Weld, *Foundations of Psychology*

Length dissolves vehemence.

Demetrius, *On Style*

Consider these nine words in alphabetical order: *fear, have, is, itself, only, the, thing, to,* and *we.* They are common and familiar. As lexical choices for sentences, they probably would not be noticed or remembered—unless rearranged in the order remembered from Franklin Roosevelt's first inaugural address, on March 4, 1933: "The only thing we have to fear is fear itself." A generation of Americans carried that statement around in their heads for decades—and many of their children and grandchildren also know the line. A contributory causal factor is the power derived in large measure from its style or form, and eloquent stylists should understand how to construct the same kinds of sentences with repetition to artic-

ulate effectively their assertions—and use contrapuntal omission for emphasis and persuasiveness, too.

STYLIZED REPETITION: POINT

Along with "four score and seven years ago," many Americans remember other words from Abraham Lincoln: "government of the people, by the people, for the people." This statement has 10 words or "tokens." But how many *different*
words, or "types," are in it? Count them: *government* (1), *of*
(2), *the* (3), *people* (4), *by* (5), *the* (used already), *people* (used
already), *for* (6), *the* (used already), and *people* (used already).
To determine the Type-Token-Ratio, or TTR, for a statement,
divide the number of different words (types) by the total
number of words (tokens). For Lincoln's memorable words, 6
types divided by 10 tokens yield a TTR of .60 as a numerical
value for that proximity of repetition. In many statistical
studies of language behavior, Type-Token-Ratios are an index
of lexical diversity, or of how many different words characterize someone's discourse; here, the TTR reveals how repetition
is a functional source of style.

Suppose a wiretap on your home telephone recorded 24
hours of your conversation, and a stenographer typed an
accurate transcript of what you said and marked off that text
into 10- or 15-word segments. After computing a Type-Token-
Ratio for each segment and then obtaining an average TTR
for all of them, an investigator likely would reach this conclusion: if you are a native speaker of English, the statistical
probability is that out of every 10 to 15 of your words, 1 of
them was repeated. That frequency—and syntactical proximity—of repetition is normative for English speakers. So for
segments of the common idiom 10 to 15 words in length, the
probable Type-Token-Ratio is .90 to .93 (some studies used 10
word segments; others used 15 word segments). In normative

conversation, we communicate well with small vocabularies. Indeed, statistical studies of how we talk on the telephone indicate that approximately 95 per cent of such talk employs no more than about 725 different words. Normative conversation is made from a relatively small vocabulary. So we *do* repeat words in idiomatic statements, and our listeners (or readers, for that matter) are accustomed to hearing *some* repetition from us. But people do not expect the proximity and symmetry of repeated words in Lincoln's "government of the people, by the people, for the people." A TTR of .60 differs significantly from .90 in so short a statement!

Some Prominent Formats

Although *some* repetition occurs in normative language behavior, several species of repeating words are deviations from the common idiom. When more words are repeated than expected, or when the *proximity* of repeated words is unexpected, particularly in symmetrical patterns, statements have style—with potential for noticeability and memorability. Moreover, although using stylized repetition requires discretion over which words to repeat (lexicon), its uncommonness is primarily a function of the proximity with which its words are arranged (syntax). Thus, Franklin Roosevelt's sentence about dire circumstances during the Great Depression was salient because *fear* was repeated in closer proximity than that to which we are accustomed. When a word or phrase is repeated in unexpectedly close proximity to its previous occurrence in a sentence, the "scheme" is called *traductio*, as in Roosevelt's eminently quotable line. *Traductio* also is used by General Douglas MacArthur when he praised the American soldier's imperative for "complete and decisive *victory— always victory, always* through the haze of their last reverberating shot."[1]

The closest proximity for repeating a word or phrase is with no different words intervening, such as in words Longfellow penned as having come from the mouth of Paul Revere, "To arms, to arms, the British are coming." This "scheme" for uncommon repetition was called *epizeuxis* by classical rhetoricians. Speakers often vary in the rhetorical sensitivity applied when using this conformation, however. In his acceptance address to the 1992 Democratic National Convention, Bill Clinton used *epizeuxis* that served little rhetorical purpose: "the rest, the rest of the world" or ""let it be, let it be." Contrast these immediate repetitions of words or phrases with that when Mr. Clinton praised his mother: "always, always she taught me to fight."

In addition to their potential novelty, these schemes achieve rhetorical power in discourse by incorporating one of the most reliable factors of attention determining the stimuli to which human beings respond: repetition. Psychologists are certain:

> The *repetition* of a stimulus helps in several ways to evoke action. First of all, a repeated stimulus is in some senses a more intense stimulus. Two shots in succession are more likely to attract our attention than one; three are perhaps more effective than two. Sometimes regular repetition helps attract attention because the first few instances sensitize us to the later ones. How often do we start to count the strokes of a clock after two or three have gone by. . . . Finally, the regular repetition of a stimulus often produces a set or expectation so strong that later members of the series are perceived the same way even when they have been changed. . . . Repetition also multiplies the chances of a stimulus' getting attention: if it misses on the first two tries, it may succeed on the third.[2]

For speakers, functional advantages of repetition are impressive. Researchers attest to the "added strength given to the stimulus by repeating it." Axiomatically, "repetition of a stimulus, up to a certain point, may have a greater effect than a single stimulus, even if the latter is fairly strong." After all, due either to the brief duration of focused attention or to poor audibility, a single presentation of an idea or point very often may go unnoticed, whereas repeated words can lodge within the "fringes of our attention." Indeed, the probability of recalling a repeated word is just about twice that of recalling a unique word, and the same advantages accrue for written words (speakers should remember that their "best words in their best orders" often appear subsequently in print). When reading words, thresholds vary inversely with frequency of prior usage, which is immediate *within the communication event* as well as the relative frequency with which these words happen to appear in human communication generally.[3]

Rule to Remember

Reserve repetition for key words. "To arms, to arms" are important words. Technically, Lincoln may have *epizeuxis* in *"that that* nation might live," but immediate repetition of *that* is a grammatical accident and does not do him as much good as when Winston Churchill called for "Victory, victory" during World War II. Communicators should use *epizeuxis*—or *any* scheme of repetition—only *purposefully* to emphasize key words for their purposes.

Uncommon repetitions such as those illustrated above are relatively subtle because they are brief in their duration for readers or listeners. At times, however, speakers will want greater emphasis from style through repetition.

Reexamine Lincoln's "government of the people. by the people, for the people." What is the "scheme" by which this line embodies repetition? Repeat the same word or phrase at

endings of successive phrases or short sentences. Parallel repetition for like endings is known traditionally as *antistrophe* or
epistrophe (these two names for this scheme are virtually interchangeable in the history of rhetorical theory). Communicators can go in the *other* direction, however, repeating the
same word or phrase at *beginnings* of successive phrases or
short sentences, as in Lincoln's "With malice toward none,
with charity for all, with firmness in the right." Symmetrical
parallelism achieved by like beginnings is called *anaphora* or
epanaphora (again, interchangeable terms).

HELPFUL HINT *Parallel repetitions often seem to sound better in
groups of three, a format known in rhetorical the-
ory as a tricolon. Lincoln's parallelism, for instance, characteristically uses repeated words or phrases in three like beginnings
or like endings.*

Rhetoricians of the past appreciated the pragmatic role of
parallel repetition (*epanaphora* is rendered from Classical
Greek into English as "I repeat"). In the *Rhetoric* (1414a), for
example, Aristotle recommended this line from Homer:
"Nireus from Syme brought three curved ships; Nireus, son of
Aglaia and of Charopus; Nireus, most beautiful of all the
Greeks who came to Troy, saving Achilles only." For "if a
good many things are said about a person, his name will have
to be mentioned pretty often; accordingly, if his name is
often mentioned, one has the impression that a good deal
has been said about him. By the use of this fallacy, Homer,
who mentions Nireus only in this single passage, makes him
important, and has preserved his memory, though in the rest
of the poem he says never a word more about him." Or, as
Demetrius observes *On Style*, "Nireus is not himself important
in the *Iliad*, and his contribution is even less so, three ships
and a few men, but Homer makes him appear important and

his contribution great. . . . Although Nireus is mentioned
only once in the action, we remember him. . . . If Homer had
said: 'Nireus, the son of Aglaia brought three ships from
Syme,' he might as well not have mentioned him."[4] Similarly,
to emphasize the American colonists' dissatisfaction with the
King of England personally more so than with Great Britain
generally, the Declaration of Independence has 13 like beginnings of "He has . . . He has . . . He has . . . " to identify the
factors justifying their revolution.

This classical advice applies to contemporary speaking.
Americans remember four words from Martin Luther King, Jr.;
they found their way onto bumper stickers and more prominent places: "I have a dream." But why were those four words
remembered from among *all* those words in King's speech,
given at the Lincoln Memorial during a Civil Rights rally?
They began several consecutive sentences and thereby
increased the likelihood that "I have a dream" would be
noticed and remembered. Some like beginnings are subtle,
however. For instance, Winston Churchill's tribute to all that
the Royal Air Force accomplished on behalf of the British
people in the early days of World War II repeated in parallel
only one word of two letters' length: "*so* much owed by *so*
many to *so* few." But whether the speaker repeats a short
word or a phrase of several words, this style conduces to
quotability and memorability.

The two patterns described above can be combined for
like beginnings *and* like endings: "You call him against yourself as a witness, you call him against the laws as a witness,
you call him against the people as a witness." As Demetrius
notes, however, "if one said: 'You call him a witness against
yourself, the laws, and the people,' the figure would disap-
pear, and so would the force of the passage."[5] The combination of *anaphora* and *antistrophe* (or *epanaphora* and *epistrophe*,
respectively) was called *conplexio*, but its user should beware.

So much repetition in a short span of discourse can be cumbersome, particularly when the repetition involves words having many syllables. In communication, a psychological phenomenon known as empathy often is operative (to empathize with someone is to assume the same physiological condition as that other person). Consider this hypothetical example of *conplexio*: "This legislation requests careful consideration; this legislation demands careful consideration; this legislation will get careful consideration." The 16 words (tokens) are founded upon 8 different words (types) for an unexpectedly low Type-Token-Ratio of .50. But to utter those words, a speaker must work hard physiologically to articulate the repeated polysyllabic words (four syllables in "le-gis-la-tion" and five syllables in "con-si-der-a-tion"). Listeners who empathize with the speaker at some subtle level are exerting effort and therefore may "tune out."

Rule to Remember

In parallel repetitions (or in any schemes for repeating words or phrases), rely on short, monosyllabic words—or perhaps words of two syllables at most, such as Lincoln's *people*. You do not want cumbersome lines that fatigue respondents.

Although highly concentrated repetition in *conplexio* can be disadvantageous, some of these statements do work well. You most likely remember one of the most quoted lines of poetry in the English language; from Gertrude Stein, its 10 tokens and 3 types yield a highly unusual TTR of .30; and the poet herself suggests why this statement about a rose is novel and thereby memorable:

> Now the poet has to work in the excitingness of pure being; he has to get back that intensity into the lan-

guage. We all know that it's hard to write poetry in a late age, and we know that you have to put some strangeness, something unexpected, into the structure of the sentence in order to bring back the vitality of the noun. Now it's not enough to be bizarre; the strangeness in the sentence structure has to come from the poetic gift, too. That's why it's doubly hard to be a poet in a late age. Now you have seen hundreds of poems about roses and you know in your bones that the rose is not there. All those songs that sopranos sing as encores about "I have a garden; oh, what a garden!" Now I don't want to put too much emphasis on that line, because it's just one line in a longer poem. But I notice that you all know it; you can make fun of it, but you know it, now listen! I'm no fool. I know that in daily life we don't go around saying "is a . . . is a . . . is a . . . is a . . . ." Yes, I'm no fool; but I think that in that line the rose is red for the first time in English poetry for a hundred years.[6]

Although her commentary is about poetry, Stein's conclusion is applicable to public speaking.

Some Caveats; Other Options

Speakers must be wary. Parallelism—whether of like endings, like beginnings, or a combination of both—is relatively easily incorporated in discourse. Indeed, many speakers lapse into these conformations almost unconsciously when drafting discourse or speaking impromptu or extemporaneously. The result can be mechanistic repetition that does not serve speakers well. In his acceptance address to the 1992 Democratic National Convention, Bill Clinton used impractical parallelism extensively, either as like beginnings, "a government that offers more empowerment . . . a government that is leaner . . . a government that . . . ," or as like endings advocating a "family policy, urban policy, labor policy, minority policy, and foreign policy." Are *government* and *policy* really important enough words to be emphasized through style? Emphasis is squandered to even greater extent with Clinton's *anaphora* or *epanaphora* about the Republican administration: "It's been hijacked by privileged, private interests. It's forgotten who really pays the bills around here. It's taking more of your money and giving you less service." Repetition of the contraction *it's* is a mechanistic one that does not serve him as well as one reminiscent of King's parallel " I have a dream." Clinton does emphasize his personal potential for leadership, however, when he founds parallel like beginnings upon "I hope . . . I hope . . . I hope . . . ." Stylized repetition should be pragmatically functional.

For all of his tactical and strategic acumen as a general, Douglas MacArthur actually may be more familiar to many Americans because of his words, some of which are remarkably memorable. During his widely quoted speech to West Point cadets, lauding "Duty, Honor, Country," MacArthur concluded by saying that his "last conscious thoughts" at the close of his life would be of "the Corps, and the Corps, and the Corps." This line achieved memorability—and poignantly so—at least for Ronald Reagan. When a Pentagon corridor was dedicated to MacArthur, President Reagan's speech on that occasion praised "the general and the general and the general" (evoking tears from both MacArthur's widow and Nancy Reagan).[7] So for all of their low TTRs and the resultant novelty conducing to emphasis and memorability, some schemes of repetition also are capable of endowing statements with emotional impact.

Another observation is in order, however, about unexpectedly low Type-Token-Ratios. In AB–BA antitheses (*urbanitas* or *chiasmus*), TTRs invariably are low. After all, key words from the first half are repeated, albeit in reversed order, in the second half. For example, 17 tokens and 9 types compose John

Kennedy's "Ask not what your country can do for you—ask what you can do for your country"; the TTR is .53 (to the nearest hundredth) with a potential novelty operative to help capture attention. Compute the Type-Token-Ratios for "When the going gets tough the tough get going" or "You can take Salem out of the country, but you can't take the country out of Salem." In addition to being short, well balanced AB–BA antitheses, these lines capitalize upon uncommon proximity of repetition to help make then noteworthy and more memorable.

Two other schemes of uncommon repetition should be in the repertoire of public speakers. One is the uncommon repetition of conjunctions, called *polysyndeton* (*poly* signifying "many" and *syndeton* meaning "connective," and recall that the six conjunctions in English are *and, or, but, for, nor,* and *yet*). The norm for using conjunctions has been carefully taught to English speakers: when listing items in a series, put a conjunction between the last two, as in "The colors of the American flag are red, white, *and* blue." But *polysyndeton* would say "red and white and blue." Or, as John Kennedy said in his inaugural address, "Where the strong are just *and* the weak secure *and* the peace preserved." Douglas MacArthur's "the Corps, and the Corps, and the Corps" also is *polysyndeton.*

In addition to potential novelty derived from repeating conjunctions, consider another possible effect of this uncommon usage. Some United States senator might have said this: "Behind me in the fight for this bill are the states of Maine, New Hampshire, Vermont, Massachusetts, and Connecticut." Inserting *and* between the last two items is the customary usage taught in schools. But imagine that senator saying this: "Behind me in this fight are the states of Maine and New Hampshire and Vermont and Massachusetts and Connecticut." The effect *is* different! Listeners may say to themselves, "Wow, *that* many?"

Traditional rhetoricians frequently praise the pragmatism of *polysyndeton*. George Campbell said that impressive "multiplicity of the circumstances" is suggested by *polysyndeton* because the persuader thereby creates "a deliberate attention to every circumstance, as being of importance." Similarly, Hugh Blair recommended sentences wherein conjunctions are "multiplied" so that the objects in between "should appear as distinct from one another as possible, and that the mind should rest, for a moment, on each object by itself."[8]

HELPFUL HINT *Whenever you as a writer or speaker want to suggest the scope or magnitude of the aspects of your subject listed in sequence, put a conjunction between each one. Simply by repeating "and . . . and . . . and . . . and . . . " you create the impression that a great deal is involved. But do not use* polysyndeton *for insignificant subject matter. Readers or listeners might have doubts about a writer or speaker who is so artificial as to bestow eloquent style upon trivial subject matter.*

Polysyndeton easily might be carried to extremes, however. That senator also could say, "Behind me in this fight are the states of Maine and New Hampshire and Vermont and Massachusetts and Connecticut and Rhode Island and New York and Pennsylvania and Delaware and . . . and . . . and . . . ." The effect is not novelty but monotony! No more than four or five repetitions of conjunctions between particulars achieve a golden mean in style.

Another species of uncommon repetition is not of words but of sounds: alliteration. The common idiom is not alliterative by beginning successive words (or words particularly close together) with the same sound. Because such statements are sufficiently salient for people, they often become bases of slogans, such as these prominent in American history: "Fifty-four-forty or fight," "Tippecanoe and Tyler too," or even the more subtle alliteration in "Remember the Maine."

Rule to Remember

Do not extend alliteration over too many words, for you may wind up with a tongue twister (which in turn likely will make listeners uncomfortable), as in "Sally sells seashells successfully by the seashore." Lincoln's alliteration, for example, typically does not extend over more than three words, as in "four *score* and *seven*" or *fathers* brought *forth*."

Choice of which sounds are repeated for alliteration should be influenced by considerations of their value as morphemes, too. For instance, *flash, flare, flame,* and *flicker* all have the common sound (fl) as a common meaning suggestive of moving light. As I. A. Richards observes, "two or more words are said to share a morpheme when they have at the same time, something in common in their meaning and something in common in their sound. The joint semantic-phonetic unit which distinguishes them is what is called a morpheme."[9] To capitalize on this aspect of language, alliterate those sounds whose morphemes complement the subject at hand. In discourse about war, alliteration with the voiced plosive (b) might be appropriate as the sound at some level makes people aware of all the martial *b* words such as *battle, bombard, batter, blitz,* or *bomb*. Similarly, the unvoiced plosive (p) as a basis for alliteration might remind people at some level of all those words which share a meaning of something re*p*ugnant to be expelled or avoided, such as *puke, putrid, repel,* or the alliterative term Vice-President Spiro Agnew coined for his political detractors: "pusillanimous pussyfooters."

Excessive recurrence of the same sound may be alleviated by "hidden" alliteration, such as that in Winston Churchill's "I have nothing to offer but blood, toil, tears, and sweat." The "t" sound is complemented by its voiced counterpart of "d" in *blood* (in order to articulate both "t" and "d," the physiology of the mouth must be in the same configuration, but "d" is voiced whereas "t" is not). As people become more proficient stylists, they begin to make phrases alliteratively as successive words are chosen almost instantaneously for their similarity in sound. If the similar sounds are vowels, the quality sometimes is called assonance, whereas repeated consonants is called consonance. For pragmatic stylists, however, repetition of sounds, as a source of more emphatic statements, is known simply as alliteration. Moreover, this source of style is combined easily with other schemes, such as Clinton's *polysyndeton* when his 1992 acceptance address lauded "family and friends and a faith that in America no one is left out."

Rule to Remember

Use schemes of repetition only for those words with semantic punch pertinent to achieving your objectives as a communicator. To repeat any other words is simply to waste the potential emphasis derived from schematic repetition—and potentially to divert emphasis from other, more significant materials for readers or listeners. Do not squander repetition on unworthy words!

In his second inaugural address, while proposing a "security shield" in space, Ronald Reagan said, "*It* wouldn't kill people, *it* would destroy weapons. *It* wouldn't militarize space, *it* would help demilitarize the arsenals of earth. *It* would render nuclear weapons obsolete." Yes, those like beginnings technically constitute *anaphora* or *epanaphora*, but *it* is impotent. Why make *it* emphatic? Contrast Ronald Reagan's use of stylized repetition with that of Winston Churchill during the darkest days of World War II, when Hitler seemed ready to cross the Channel and invade England: "We shall fight on the beaches, we shall fight on the landing grounds, we shall fight in the fields and in the streets, we shall fight in the hills . . . ." "We shall fight" merits repetition. And surely a key word in Lincoln's Gettysburg Address *is* "people."

The Classical Greeks had a word for the functional quality of style founded in many cases upon repetition: *onkos*. Aristotle believed a desired effect of style was the suggestion to respondents of a "bulk" or "mass" that in turn bestows "elevation" or "dignity" upon the points that a speaker would emphasize.[10] Whether from repetitions that place important points in the parallelism of like beginnings or like endings (or the combination of both) or even that more subtle repetition of conjunctions, speakers can heighten the impressiveness of their subject matter.

In the final analysis about schemes of repetition, an axiom is in order: eloquent stylists are pragmatists. After drafting any statement embodying stylized repetition, look at the words thus emphasized. Do they truly merit respondents' attention? If not, delete the impotent repetition and find more worthy words as bases of style. Similarly, at some point, repetition becomes obtrusive. Lincoln typically did not exceed patterns founded upon three elements. John Kennedy used a sequence founded upon four elements:

> Let both sides explore what problems unite us instead of belaboring those problems which divide us. Let both sides, for the first time, formulate serious and precise proposals for the inspection and control of arms—and bring the absolute power to destroy other nations under the absolute control of all nations. Let both sides seek to invoke the wonders of science instead of its terrors. . . . Let both sides unite to heed in all corners of the earth the command of Isaiah—to "undo the heavy burdens . . . let the oppressed go free."

Admittedly, this sequence incorporates several antitheses, between *unite* and *divide, explore* and *belabor, absolute power* and *absolute control,* as well as between *wonders* and *terrors,* to designate aspects of a combined venture. But stylized repetition of "let both sides" emphasizes the spirit in which problems should be solved.

With anything beyond four repetitions, however, communicators may push their luck (although Martin Luther King, Jr., succeeded with more successive repetitions of "I have a dream," the successive repetition of "I" reinforced *his* position of leadership in the Civil Rights movement). In the psychology of communication, "change is the most basic and significant attention value," and "one of the most reliable findings" of experimentation about attention is that "with repeated exposures novel objects rather quickly lose their power to elicit approach."[11] At some point, repeated words are no longer emphatic but monotonous. Take a clock that ticks into a quiet room and set it on a desk or table in front of you; concentrate attention on the sound of the ticking. Two things will happen. First, for the first several ticks you will think that the sounds are getting progressively louder. They are not, actually, but as the ear drum adapts to the same sound, the stimulus is processed more efficiently. So with less pressure needed from each sound as stimulus for the ear drum, successive ticks seems louder.

HELPFUL HINT *In oral discourse, each successive repetition of a word or phrase may seem louder to a listener— even if it is not. So on television, for instance, where a "cool," restrained image is desired, you may not want to increase volume as a speaker (and cause consternation to engineers in the control room as well). Emphasis derived from parallel repetition could be the appropriate counterpart of raising your voice.*

But after a few more ticks of that clock, the second phase of response takes over. With excessive repetitions, *any* stimulus becomes monotonous; and try as hard as you might to pay attention to the ticking of the clock, you will not "hear" it after a while. The human being does not like an unchanging stimulus pattern after a while; and if stimuli do not change, people will alter their perceptions. In your psychology textbook, the chapter on perception likely used the drawing of what appears at first to be a white vase against a black background. After staring at it for a few seconds, you then "see" two faces in black silhouette against a white background.

Rule to Remember

No matter what species of stylized repetition is used, its overuse can be disadvantageous. Repeating a word or phrase too much for style yields only monotony.

But eloquent stylists may inject subtle variation into parallel repetition that nevertheless retains symmetry for the statement. Consider this *epistrophe* or *antistrophe* from Franklin Roosevelt's statement about a world founded upon four essential human freedoms:

> The first is freedom of speech and expression everywhere in the world. The second is freedom of every person to worship God in his own way everywhere in the world. The third is freedom from want, which translated into world terms means economic understandings which will secure to every nation a healthy, peacetime life for its inhabitants everywhere in the world. The fourth is freedom from fear, which translated into world terms means a world-wide reduction in armaments to such a point and in such a thorough fashion that no nation will be in a position to commit an act of physical aggression against any neighbor, *anywhere* in the world.

The subtle variation from the clearly established pattern—while still retaining symmetry of form—constitutes a discrepancy from what is expected and even more novelty for emphasis of the last phrase.

COUNTERPOINT: OMISSION

Try another experiment now. Get some paper and write a paragraph that describes your experiences since awakening this morning. Write and complete this paragraph in exactly 90 seconds, composing in complete sentences with subjects and predicates, forgetting about neatness. Your objective is to provide as much detail and information as you can about those experiences. When 90 seconds are up, stop. Then determine the exact length of the paragraph in total number of words.

For this experiment, assume that your paragraph described the most emotionally moving experience you have had in many years. Your soul was touched in a way unlike any other experiences, so you must relate that information immediately to your dearest friend—who at this time is working on an oil drilling rig off the coast of Borneo. Your friend cannot be reached by e-mail or telephone, and an airmail letter still would take weeks to reach that person. Because your information is so important, however, you go to a telegraph office. After learning the destination of your message, the person in charge indicates your statement will go by transPacific cable to Hong Kong, subsequently to Singapore, then by a relay to Sarawak, and finally by native outrigger canoe to the offshore platform—at a cost of $15 per word! You do not have enough cash; your checkbook is in disarray; and you dare not offer your credit card number at this time (the telegraph office might make that telephone call to find you over your limit). Upon looking closer in your wallet, however, you find enough money to send the telegram—*if* you reduce the number of words by one third. So rewrite your paragraph using complete sentences with subjects and predicates and retain *all* of its information—but with one-third fewer words. For example, a 90-second version might have said this:

> It was 7:00 A.M. when the alarm from my clock awakened me from my deep sleep. I got out of bed and stumbled with my eyes half-closed into the bathroom. I shaved, and then I took a shower and got dressed. All of these activities were taking me longer to perform than expected so I did not have time to eat any breakfast as I customarily do. It was clear to me that I would have only enough time to drive to the office and to be there on time when it opened. (94 words)

A second version with the same content or information has over one-third fewer words:

> At 7:00 A.M., the clock alarm awakened me from deep sleep. I got out of bed, stumbled with half-closed eyes into the bathroom, shaved, showered, and dressed. These activities took longer than expected. No time remained for my customary breakfast. Clearly, I only had time to drive and be at my office when it opened. (55 words)

From first drafts, sentence lengths typically can be reduced to fewer words—without sacrificing content or information, and participation in this writing exercise should demonstrate a principle about customary language behavior: people typically use more words than absolutely necessary to communicate. They do so as "an insurance against mistakes," for as George Miller observes, the extra words allow discourse to be "more dependable under adverse circumstances."

> A large degree of interdependence among the successive units of a message means that parts of the message can be lost or distorted without causing a disruption of communication. Any missing portions can be supplied by the receiver on the basis of the surrounding portions,

on the basis of the contextual cues. . . . And since our
nervous systems seem to absorb new information
slowly, if at all, we suffer little inconvenience in going
slower while we gain considerably in reliability.[12]

Thus, if we use more words than the bare minimum, static on
the telephone line or waiters dropping a tray in a hotel ball-
room or some other intrusion will not prevent us from being
understood. For respondents still comprehend the gist of the
message from all the other words that make our sentences
longer than absolutely necessary. That is the common idiom.

Exceptionally short sentences are deviations from the common idiom and a source of style—with resultant potential for
novelty and emphasis. During World War II, U.S. Navy pilot
Donald F. Mason was flying a patrol bomber over the Atlantic
Ocean on January 8, 1942, and searching for German submarines. He *might* have described his ensuing encounter this
way: "I sighted a submarine on the surface, and I attacked and
sank it." That would be the common and familiar idiom.
Instead, at least as reported in the newspapers, he sent this
radio message: "Sighted sub; sank same." So short a statement
deviated from the common idiom; and although its alliteration
helped, the statement was noticed and quoted widely because
of its novelty. Notice, however, that the exceptionally terse
sentence attributed to Mason nevertheless embodies a normative tendency of language users. That is, whenever a polysyllabic word is used frequently, its utterance is made easier by
truncating the word into one syllable. *Submarine* becomes *sub*;
automobile becomes *auto*; or *telephone* becomes *phone*.[13] But
even the truncated word, in this case *sub,* contributed to the
clipped, terse quality of the statement.

THE ADVANTAGES OF CONCISENESS

To classical rhetoricians, "explicit conciseness" was called *brevitas*, or the expression of an idea "by the very minimum of

essential words."[14] Perhaps the best single synonym for this quality of usage is terseness, whereby sentences are stripped of extraneous words to achieve the absolute bare minimum number of words necessary to communicate intended meanings.

Rule to Remember

Be careful! Messages can be too terse. In efforts to create exceptionally short sentences, someone can eliminate words that are essential for communication effectiveness. If you have not received one already, someday you might receive a telegram wherein the writer had one eye on the sentences being composed and another eye on the number of dollars available to send it. So many words were eliminated that after several rereadings, you were still unsure of what the telegram was telling you.

To achieve *brevitas* or terseness, choices are made about which words to omit, yes, but this source of style has a significant, syntactical dimension derived from the act of omitting some words: the omissions serve to place kernel elements of the sentence closer and closer together.

In rhetorical theory, a widely recommended scheme of omission is *asyndeton* (*a* signifying "without" and *syndeton* signifying "connective"). In English, when listing items in series, customary usage dictates that the last two are separated by a conjunction (this is the same rule for normative usage that makes *polysyndeton* a deviation from the common idiom). If that conjunction is omitted, however, the communicator has deviated from the common idiom, as in this example from the *Rhetorica Ad Herennium*: "Indulge your father, obey your relatives, gratify your friends, submit to the laws."[15] Imagine Abraham Lincoln in a contemporary composition class, turning in the Gettysburg Address as an assignment. The teacher looking at the last sentence might say,

"Abe, if I have told you once, I have told you 10 times: when you list items in series, put a conjunction between the last two and say 'government of the people, by the people, *and* for the people.' You made the same mistake in 'We cannot dedicate, we cannot consecrate, we cannot hallow this ground.' Oh Abe, what am I going to do about you?" Omitting conjunctions, specifically, is another way of deviating from the common idiom and helping to achieve terseness.

Although the common idiom typically uses more words than necessary to make statements, several species of uncommon usage discussed previously make statements even longer. Parallel repetitions lengthen statements. For example, "government of, by, and for the people" uses fewer words than Lincoln's stylized version. Antitheses also make sentences longer, for they essentially embody heretofore *unstated* opposites. Thus, someone may want to say that something is a blessing; but to make the antithesis for the statement, words must be added: "not a curse but a blessing." And John Kennedy's essential point was that Americans should "ask what you can do for your country." If Abraham Lincoln's Gettysburg Address were rewritten with the characteristically antithetical style of John Kennedy (and Ted Sorensen), for instance, the speech in final form would be longer—although its content would remain substantially the same.

Brevitas therefore constitutes an effective *counterpoint* to sentences having other syntactical sources of style. Amid utterances deriving style from deviations that add words, a particularly terse statement stands out. Thus, in addition to its novelty, terseness can constitute relief from more weighty parts of discourse. Terseness also may be particularly appropriate in two, precise sentences of your discourse—the first and the last, which are the ones to achieve emphasis with the least amount of effort exerted by listeners or readers. To open a formal statement, I prefer a terse sentence. For example, some of my essays in scholarly journals open with a three-word sentence, such as "Style is functional," or even a two-word sentence, "Historians persuade." After all, scholars do not expect research reports to use sentences of two or three words length (nor do you, for that matter, so I began this book with a two-word sentence: "Words work"). Final sentences also may warrant *brevitas*. At the surrender of Japan in 1945, General Douglas MacArthur spoke to conclude the cere-monies on the deck of the battleship *Missouri* in Tokyo Bay. He might have ended with something like this: "Now that the formal procedures of this meeting are completed, we are adjourned." He said, instead, "These proceedings are closed." Indeed, two of MacArthur's other statements that are widely remembered from World War II are terse proclamations: ("I shall return," after arriving in Australia before the Japanese overran the Philippine Islands in 1942, and "I have returned," when wading ashore from a landing barge when American armed forces returned to the Philippines in 1944). But as suggested by the effectiveness of statements such as MacArthur's, *brevitas* has another potential pragmatic effect.

The Classical Greeks had another maxim about style in discourse: "length dissolves vehemence." As Demetrius observed in his treatise *On Style*, "it is both more forceful and more violent to express much in few words. It was the force-fulness of the Spartans that made them brief in speech. Orders are always short and brief, and every master is mono-syllabic to his slaves, whereas supplications and lamentations are lengthy . . . as old men are verbose because they are weak"[16] To paraphrase that classical criterion, the more a con-temporary speaker would suggest decisiveness, passion, or depth of feeling about a subject, the fewer words should express that idea. In a school classroom, someone might be talking consistently to another student in a loud, disruptive manner. A teacher could say, "If you persist in making noise which disturbs other people's concentration, you know, just one more time, I will have to ask you to leave the room." Or, that teacher might say, "Once more, out!" The latter, terse version is more emphatic and projects decisiveness. Somehow, "I came; I saw; I conquered" *is* more decisive and passionate than its idiomatic counterpart with *and* inserted between the last two elements.

Think further about this notion of style and its persuasive paramessage. Many people remember another line from John Kennedy: *"Ich bin ein Berliner."* That statement was made in Berlin at an event heavy with emotional significance, and Kennedy's projection of passion was appropriate (although many residents of Berlin might have thought that Kennedy's use of the word *Berliner* was a reference to one of their favorite pastries that had that word for its name). When President Ronald Reagan spoke at Bitburg, Germany, for an event of potentially similar significance, he said this:

> Twenty-two years ago, President John F. Kennedy went to the Berlin Wall and proclaimed that he, too, was a Berliner. Today, freedom-loving people around the world must say: I am a Berliner, I am a Jew in a world still threatened by anti-Semitism, I am an Afghan, and I am a prisoner of the Gulag, I am a refugee in a crowded boat foundering off the coast of Vietnam, I am a Laotian, a Cambodian, a Cuban, and a Miskito Indian in Nicaragua. I, too, am a potential victim of totalitarianism.

President Reagan's counterpart had too many hypothetical referents for "I," which some people might hear, literally, as "I Ronald Reagan . . . I Ronald Reagan. . . ." Moreover, this line, too, seems to project that very quality which Demetrius perceived as undesirable: "The writer who deals with a trivial subject in weighty language is like a man who pretends to qualities he does not possess, undeterred by his lack of them, or like a man who boasts about trifles."[17]

Rule to Remember

Brevitas is appropriate in rhetorical situations when content warrants projecting decisiveness, passion, or depth of emotion. For example, during the 1988 presidential campaign, the vice-presidential candidates—elderly Lloyd Bentson (Democrat) and youthful Dan Quayle (Republican) appeared in a TV debate. After Quayle's attempt to identify himself with John Kennedy in the voters' minds, Bentsen uttered four words with decisive, epigrammatic style that made them eminently quotable for several weeks afterwards: "You're no John Kennedy."

Any draft of a document can be edited stylistically to achieve terse sentences. But this is *not* a blanket endorsement of *brevitas* as a quality that should prevail in every sentence of discourse. Length is important, too. After all, discourse must present as much content as necessary to explain or prove its point—reliably. Eliminating words may eliminate important content. Moreover, impulses to achieve power from words expressed in antitheses or parallel repetitions are thwarted when communicators strive for *brevitas* throughout their statements. As noted earlier, stylized repetitions and antitheses invariably lead to using more words than absolutely necessary. Pragmatic stylists want to achieve functional eloquence whereby the length and weightiness of other sources of style have their counterpoint in terseness for relief, emotional punch, and decisiveness.

Some Bases of Brevitas

Several, specific techniques help attain terseness. Actually, all sentences may profit from applying the following guidelines, but these techniques used by public speakers (or writers for a wide range of discourse) are conducive to attaining *brevitas*.

Perfecting Plurals

Write in the plural rather than the singular. Because of articles such as *a* and *the,* sentences in the singular invariably require more words. In nine words, "A boy prefers a football as a Christmas present." The plural uses six words: "Boys prefer footballs as Christmas presents," for a 33 percent reduction in word length. Generally, writing in the plural omits articles, and the plural—if the sense permits—is more categorical as well, like axioms or definitive statements suggesting writers' decisiveness. The plural also helps writers avoid problems evolving from sexist language, such as "he or she" or the cumbersome "he/she" and "his/her." Consider "He or she may return the product to get his or her money back." The plural, "They may return the product to get their money back," reduces 14 words to 10, a 28 percent decrease in length. Or three words, *men and women,* can become one word: *people.* Apply this principle for the following sentence: "A wife and husband view the arrival of a first child with excitement."

Deleting Evil Expletives

For *brevitas,* expletives do *not* refer to unseemly words such as *damn.* In grammar, expletives change writing from active to passive forms. In eight words, you might write, "There are three factors that cause the problem"; only five words are needed for "Three factors cause the problem," for a 37 percent decrease in length. Ten words say, "It was the quality of his voice that irritated me"; seven say "The quality of his voice irritated me." Rewrite the following sentence deleting expletives (and using the punctuation mark, the apostrophe, to show possession): "It was a case of pregame jitters that caused the player to make mistakes."

Applying Admirable Adverbs

Although some political candidates get mileage out of the *L* word, liberal, all communicators can get mileage out of "ly" words, adverbs. Expletive constructions often use nouns which, when changed to adverbs, reduce length. Look at the underlined noun in the nine words "It is with <u>pride</u> that I announce my candidacy." Length becomes five words when the noun becomes an adverb: "Proudly, I announce my candidacy," a 44 percent length reduction. Or, ten words in "It was with diligence that he prepared for the trial" become six in "He diligently prepared for the trial," a 40 percent length reduction. Many words can be both nouns and verbs, such as *cause* or *influence,* and changing that grammatical mode may yield shorter sentences. Eight words in "Smoking is a cause of discomfort to others" become five in "Smoking causes discomfort to others" (and with the apostrophe of "others' discomfort," another word may be deleted). Practice changing noun constructions to adverbs in the following sentence: "He changed the tire with efficiency and resumed the trip with elation."

Cultivating Cool Colons

Among punctuation marks, colons create compact writing. Consider "Overeating, smoking, and lack of exercise are three factors that contribute to heart disease" in contrast to "Three factors contribute to heart disease: overeating, smoking, and lack of exercise." Constructions with colons seem more decisive, suggesting control of subject matter. Practice incorporating a colon in this sentence: "Willingness to revise and desire to be eloquent are the two factors leading to better writing."

To practice these principles now, rewrite the following paragraph reducing 172 words to 93 at most for a 40 percent decrease—with *no* loss of essential detail and information:

It is with fear that I approach this task. The teachers of English in my high school were inept when it came to the teaching of composition. They were lacking in formal training in rhetoric, and this made them uncertain of what to teach. The advice of Classical rhetoricians about the subject of style that is eloquent had been ignored, and this is unfortunate. Several of those theorists had sound advice about the qualities of sentences that are conducive to the memorability of the statements of a writer. The three other factors that compound the problem are the size of a class, the number of the papers that a teacher is engaged in grading, and the poor attitude of a student toward writing. There is another factor that is a substantial influence upon the ability of a student to write well. This is the amount of time that a student spends in the watching of TV instead of the reading that should be done to know the models to emulate with diligence.

Public speakers, or any communicators for that matter, sooner or later will be in rhetorical situations wherein the overall length of their statements is a crucial factor. Speakers often are limited to a certain number of minutes within which they must articulate their views; for many species of written communication, length is just as much a pivotal variable (some letters to the editor of a magazine or newspaper, for instance, must be reduced substantially in length before they are publishable). All of the above techniques for shortening sentences can be applied in drafting a statement so as to get the greatest "mileage" out of the few words to which communicators are limited in some situations. And even if length of a speaker's statement is not limited as severely, employing the above techniques to achieve *brevitas* overall serves to allow more content and information to be said in the same length of time.

In conclusion, particularly terse sentences—when used sparingly or judiciously—have potential advantages in public speaking. Not only can they bestow novelty upon some sentences for resultant emphasis but also they can project the passion or decisiveness of communicators. Thus, *brevitas* is an effective counterpoint to the longer sentences stylized in other ways through *onkos* to lend power to public speaking as well as any mode of communication.

NOTES

1. For an overview of research about repetition in the common idiom, as well as the possible ways to deviate from those norms, see my essay, "The Essential Schemes of Syntax: An Analysis of Rhetorical Theory's Recommendations for Uncommon Word Orders," *Quarterly Journal of Speech* 55 (April 1969): 161–168.

2. Edwin G. Boring, Herbert S. Langfeld, and Harry Porter Weld, *Foundations of Psychology* (New York: John Wiley and Sons, 1948): 219–220.

3. Jon Eisenson, J. Jeffrey Auer, and John V. Irwin, *The Psychology of Communication* (New York: Appleton-Century-Crofts, 1963): 239; Giles W. Gray and Claude M. Wise, *The Bases of Speech*, third ed. (New York: Harper and Row, 1959): 416; Winston L. Brembeck and William S. Howell, *Persuasion: A Means of Social Control* (New York: Prentice-Hall, 1952): 276; Richard L. Solomon and Leo Postman, "Frequency of Usage as a Determinant of Recognition Threshold for Words," *Journal of Experimental Psychology* 43 (1952): 198; Nancy C. Waugh, "Immediate Memory as a Function of Repetition," *Journal of Verbal Learning and Verbal Behavior* 2 (1963): 109. Nevertheless, the threshold of recognition also is more efficient according to "the relative frequency with which that word occurs in the Thorndike-Lorge word counts." See Davis Howes and Richard L. Solomon, "Visual Duration Threshold as a Function of Word-Probability," *Journal of Experimental Psychology* 41 (1951): 410.

4. Aristotle *Rhetoric* iii. 12, and Demetrius *On Style* 6, in the translation by G.M.A. Grube (Toronto: University of Toronto Press, 1961).

5. Demetrius *On Style* 268.

6. Gertrude Stein, *Four in America* (New Haven: Yale University Press, 1947): v. Some people recall this particular line of poetry as beginning with "a," and that incorrect memory has 11 tokens and 3 types for more unusual TTR of .27.

7. "Interview with Mrs. Douglas MacArthur," 37. In the Douglas MacArthur Archives, Norfolk Virginia. Or see my Chapter 5 in Bernard K. Duffy and Ronald H. Carpenter, *Douglas MacArthur, Warrior as Wordsmith* (Westport, CT: Greenwood, 1997).

8. George Campbell, *The Philosophy of Rhetoric*, ed. Lloyd F. Bitzer (Carbondale: Southern Illinois University Press, 1963): 368; Hugh Blair, *Lectures on Rhetoric and Belles Lettres* (London, 1787), Vol. I, Lecture XII: 292–293.

9. I. A. Richards, *The Philosophy of Rhetoric* (London: Oxford University Press, 1936): 57–63.

10. See the more recent translation of Aristotle's *Rhetoric* by George A. Kennedy (New York: Oxford University Press, 1991): 233.

11. See, for instance, Eisenson, Auer, and Irwin, 239, as well as Judson S. Brown, *Motivation: A Systematic Reinterpretation* (New York: Ronald Press Company, 1959): 332.

12. George A. Miller, *Language and Communication*, rev. ed. (New York: McGraw-Hill, 1963): 103. See also my discussion of this tendency in "The Essential Schemes of Syntax," *ibid.*

13. Miller, *Language and Communication*, 89–90.

14. See the *Rhetorica Ad Herennium*, for instance, translation by Harry Caplan (London: William Heineman Ltd., 1954): iv, 54, 68.

15. *Rhet. Ad Her.* iv, 30, 41.

16. Demetrius *On Style* 241–242.

17. Demetrius, 119.

6 THE POWER OF PLACEMENT

Form . . . *is an arousing and fulfillment of desires. A work has form insofar as one part of it leads a reader to another part, to be gratified by the experience.*

Kenneth Burke, *Counter-Statement*

When Senator Everett Dirksen died, his stature warranted a funeral ceremony in the Capitol Rotunda. During his eulogy of Dirksen, then President Richard Nixon said this:

> A politician knows that more important than the bill that is proposed is the law that is passed. A politician knows that his friends are not always his allies, and that his adversaries are not his enemies. A politician knows how to make the process of democracy work and loves the intricate workings of the democratic system. A politician knows not only how to count votes but how to make his vote _____.

Count was not printed above, but you *know* it fills the blank, and you know that primarily because of the stylistic *form* of that utterance. This chapter will explain why and how to control psychological responses of people to anticipate accurately what speakers will say next. Moreover, that power will be explained not only in terms of what happens within sentences but also in terms of the overall organization for an effective speech.

Do another experiment. Ask people to fill in the blank immediately after you say "Chickens cackle and ducks ____." Although someone might say, "waddle," most people will respond with "quack." Try "Apples grow on ____." The likely response will be "trees." Next, try "The door was hermetically ____." People who know the meaning of *hermetically* will say, "sealed," for no other word is accurate (*closed* will not do because *hermetically* means "air-tight"). For another, essential trial for the experiment, have people respond to "The boy was ____." You probably will get as many different words as the number of people you ask. For some sentences, accurate predictions about completing words are impossible; but for your pragmatic purposes as a speaker and stylist, you often will "engineer" responses so people know what your final word or phrase is—*before* it occurs (engineers plan components and their functions to obtain predictable results just that way). A body of knowledge called Information Theory offers bases for understanding this pragmatic goal of communication.

REDUNDANCY AND INFORMATION

In some composition course, your teacher may have proclaimed one of your papers to be "Redundant!"—and may have given you a reduced grade. Your teacher used that word to denote excessive restatement. From the perspective of Information Theory, however, *redundant* has a different meaning. After "Chickens cackle and ducks," the word *quack* offers little information. Because of the words beginning the statement, *quack* was sufficiently predictable that you knew the word *before* it was presented. Similarly, after "The door was hermetically," the word *sealed* is predictable to someone knowing what *hermetically* means. When *sealed* then appears, it offers *no* new information for a respondent. But what follows "The boy was" is unpredictable and thereby *does* contain a considerable amount of information. So the more predictable a word is, the less information it provides; conversely, the less predictable a word is, the more information it provides. In the vocabulary of Information Theory, the more a word is predictable, the more it is redundant. Thus, for some eloquent style in discourse, redundancy does not mean being repetitive but rather helping people anticipate accurately how statements end (although when a predicted or redundant word does appear, it does "repeat," in a sense, what was known already).

Stylistically derived redundancy also is understood in terms of alternatives. To complete a sentence with one word after "The boy was _____," the number of alternatives from which the next word can be chosen is immense. Possibilities include *fat, slender, fast, slow, blue, smart, stupid, running, swimming* or any number of other choices that make meaningful statements. After "the door was hermetically _____," however, only one alternative is most accurate: *sealed*; and although *waddle* is possible after "chickens cackle and ducks _____," the more likely completion, because of the context, is *quack*. So the greater the number of alternatives from which a successive word is chosen, the more information it provides; the fewer the number of alternatives from which a successive word was chosen, the less information it conveys.

Yes, speeches (or any discourse, for that matter) should convey "information" in the commonly accepted sense of that word. Pragmatically, however, public speakers should understand that effectiveness is derived not simply by the amount of material conveyed but by the *reliability* of the process to evoke meanings accurately and efficiently. Suppose those earlier sentence completion experiments used sophisticated equipment, whereby stimuli such as "The door was hermetically _____" were flashed on a screen by a slide projector and held before respondents for minuscule amounts of time before the screen went blank. Subjects for the experiment would be seated at an Audience Sequential Analyzer, which is basically an electronic writing surface; and when a special pencil touches it to begin writing a response to a stimulus, experimenters measure the elapsed time, in hundredths of a second, between the screen going blank and subjects beginning to write the word to fill the blank. A word in response to "Chickens cackle and ducks _____" is written significantly faster than *whatever* word is written after "The boy was _____." Axiomatically, speed of response is related directly to numbers of alternatives that must be considered when making choices. The fewer the number of alternatives from which a next word is chosen to make a sentence, the more predictable and therefore redundant it is. Numerous studies support an incontrovertible law: in the context of Information Theory, increased redundancy makes statements easier to process perceptually and psychologically—and more reliable in communicating meaning accurately.[1] So despite earlier reservations about reducing "information" or being "redundant," this new perspective should influence choices whereby words work most effectively.

Actually, the common idiom is redundant. During telephone conversations, for instance, static or other extraneous noise might cause some communicators' words to be unheard. Nevertheless, listeners likely comprehend substantial parts—if not all of those messages—because the contexts afforded by other words in the statement allow accurate predictions about what was missing. Sometimes, contexts are derived from one word, such as *hermetically* dictating *sealed,* or semantic contexts are established by several words, such as "After listening to the morning news and weather report on the radio, the man who was just leaving for work decided to wear a raincoat and take along an _____." A listener might miss *umbrella* at the conclusion of the sentence—but nevertheless know it was the final word. The redundancy of *umbrella* evolves from the *semantic* meaning of the previous words, however. Therefore, the listener's prior learning and unique experiences determined whether or not the missing word was predictable. That person would know that the morning news likely contained a weather report, which typically announces the probability of rain that day; at a more subtle level, *an* indicates that the next word begins with a vowel, thereby eliminating many words that might have been considered as possibilities to fill the blank.

Eloquent stylists can achieve predictability regardless of unique prior learning and experiences of their readers or listeners, however. The sources of stylistic redundancy are the *syntactical* patterns conducing to predictability with positive influence upon ease and accuracy of responses—regardless of content and what respondents know or do not know as specific information. For these purposes, communicators, as speakers or writers, establish patterns that create perceptual sets on the part of respondents, which in turn cause perceptual selectivity characterized by "greater promptness, speed of execution, energy, or magnitude"; and an audience's accurate predictive response as a "function of the probability of that signal" is to large extent "not a theory but a demonstrable fact."[2]

Reexamine the four sentences quoted at the onset of this chapter. You knew the concluding word for President Nixon's statement was *count* because the paragraph embodied a formal pattern: a patently clear sequence of antitheses. Essentially, the first two sentences used double antitheses; the third sentence was an AB–BA reversal; and after that entire series of opposites in juxtaposition, you were conditioned for still another set of opposites to complete the pattern. The same effect is attainable *within* a single sentence, such as "Our plan helps the rich and poor, black and white, young and ___." Note, however, that predictability is not as likely when someone hears or reads "Our plan helps the young and _____." A respondent might think of *active*. But when several antitheses in sequence establish a pattern, respondents "learn" from form the content that completes the sequence.

Rule to Remember

When trying to achieve redundancy through antitheses in sequence, the more that every antithesis evolves from juxtaposing antonyms the more efficient and accurate the response at the end of the series. After all, a word may have several opposites buy *only one* antonym.

Word association experiments suggest that although people usually make synonymous pairings, seldom-used antonymical pairings are faster. In response to hearing *ocean*, someone likely will say a synonymous word such as *sea* or *water* or even an exact name such as *Atlantic*. In response to *war*, someone typically will respond with *battle, conflict,* or *soldier*, but a statistically unlikely *peace* in response to *war* actually would be a faster response.[3] Again, efficiency is a function of alternatives. *War* can call forth many synonymous words but only one antonym. So reconsider *count* at the conclusion of the antitheses quoted at the beginning of this chapter. In addition to paying attention because of emphasis derived from novelty, that person does so with psychological efficiency and an accurate anticipation that is fulfilled.

THE PERSUASIVE POWER OF FORM

We appreciate anticipations that are fulfilled. Moreover, those anticipations can be stimulated and then satisfied primarily by syntactical form of a statement more so than its ideational content. As Kenneth Burke observes, "*form* . . . is an arousing and fulfillment of desires. A work has form insofar as one part of it leads a reader to another part, to be gratified by the experience." Moreover, form, "having to do with the creation and gratification of needs, is 'correct' in so far as it gratifies the needs which it creates."[4] In psychological terminology, people prefer "closure" (sometimes spelled "clozure"). That is, people do not like incomplete configurations, such as this one flashed on a screen for a fraction of a second:

Someone likely would report "seeing" a circle or a ball; for when confronted with incomplete configurations, people tend to "fill in the blanks" and perceive what is anticipated as a more likely, complete stimulus. Moreover, people confronted with incomplete configurations typically try initially to resolve them to grasp their meaning, as in the following example of a word as it might be printed with broken type and insufficient ink:

This human need for closure nevertheless may trick us. Try another experiment. Ask someone to pronounce what they hear spelled aloud as *M-A-C-T-A-V-I-S-H*. That person will utter a Scottish name. Ask that person immediately to pronounce what these letters spell: *M-A-C-B-E-T-H*. Another Scottish name will be forthcoming. Then note that person's response to *M-A-C-D-O-N-A-L-D*. Finally, ask that same individual immediately to pronounce what these letters spell: *M-A-C-H-I-N-E-R-Y*. Because of an anticipatory "set," the person likely "heard" another Scottish name beginning with "Mac" rather than equipment called "machinery." People tend to perceive what they *expect* to perceive and not necessarily what is there as reality.

As a result of a wide range of experiences, from childhood into adulthood, people acquire "sets" that alter their perceptions of stimuli. Racial prejudices often work this way. Some years ago, experimentation at a private university (whose student body was predominantly "WASP," that is, white, Anglo-Saxon, Protestant) demonstrated this likelihood. Students were shown pen and ink drawings and allowed to view them for only a short duration of time. The drawings then were taken away, and students wrote paragraphs describing what they "saw." One drawing showed two men facing one another on a subway car. One of them, a Caucasian, held up an open straight razor; the other person was an African-American. After viewing this drawing for an instant, students then described what they had "seen." Too often, Caucasian students "saw" the African-American holding the razor, and that man was not just holding the razor but "threatening" or "robbing" the Caucasian man. Our perceptions are not always accurate, and resultant closures that people achieve in response to mere words potentially are subject to a wide range of variation, much of which might be detrimental to speakers' rhetorical objectives.

For stylists seeking to exert power through public speaking, the notion of accurate closure derived from stylistic redundancy has pragmatic applications. Persuasion can complement perceptual and psychological efficiency of responses achieved simply on behalf of listeners' accuracy of comprehension. Consider this sentence: "He who controls Berlin controls Germany; and he who controls Germany controls Europe; and he who controls Europe controls the _____." You did not have to read the word *world,* yet you knew how the statement would resolve. To explain the effectiveness of this construction, Kenneth Burke suggests that "by the time you arrive at the second of its three stages, you feel how it is destined to develop—and on the level of purely formal assent you would collaborate to round out its symmetry by spontaneously willing its completion and perfection as an utterance." And Burke regards this function of style as a source of "identification," which in its ultimate persuasive effect can be described as "consubstantiality" or "acting together" that can occur "regardless of content." His oft-quoted advice is that "you persuade a man only insofar as you can talk his language." For unsophisticated speakers, that statement might suggest endorsement of idiomatic syntax. But "formal" identification is founded instead upon *stylistic* syntax and those options of communicators in favor of word orders that are *"deviations from norms."* Consider *"we do this,* but *they* on the other hand *do that; we* stay *here,* but *they* go *there; we* look *up,* but *they* look *down,* etc." Burke's account of how these sequential antitheses function is a tribute to the persuasive efficacy of stylistically derived redundancy.

> Once you grasp the trend of the form, it invites participation regardless of subject matter. Formally, you will find yourself swinging along with the succession of antitheses, even though you may not agree with the proposition that is being presented in this form. Or it may even be an opponent's proposition which you resent—yet for the duration of the statement itself you might "help him out" to the extent of yielding to the formal development, surrendering to its symmetry as such. Of course, the more violent your original resistance to the proposition, the weaker will be your degree of "surrender" by "collaborating" with the form. But in cases where a decision is still to be reached, a yielding to the form prepares for assent to the matter identified with it. Thus, you are drawn to the form, not in your capacity as a partisan, but

because of some "universal" appeal in it. And this attitude of assent may then be transferred to the matter
which happens to be associated with the form.[5]

Similarly, Longinus, a classical critic of rhetorical style,
observed that elation wherein the audience feels as though "it
were not merely receiving, but were itself creatively partici-
pating" in the assertion being advanced (another translation
reads that an audience feels a "joy and pride" as if it had
"originated" the idea).[6] Of this originally Longinian concep-
tion Burke asks, "Could we not say that, in such cases, the
audience is exalted by the assertion because it has the feel of
collaborating in the assertion?"

Many people operate with a simplistic paradigm: persuaders say something and persuadees then agree (the persuaders hope). But recall "He who controls Berlin controls Germany" and so forth, whereby listeners complete that sequence
with *world* even *before* the speaker says, "world." When *world*
then is uttered, the persuader agrees with a conclusion reached
already in persuadees' minds. That is the best kind of persuasion, as advertisers found out when cigarette commercials
could be televised. First, they repeated their slogan for several
weeks as an AB–BA antithesis: "You can take Salem out of the
country, but you can't take the country out of Salem." Then
they changed the commercial, saying only, "You can take
Salem out of the country but"—followed by the ringing of a
little bell. Like millions of Pavlov's dogs, all intellectually sali-
vating, Americans said in their own minds, "You can't take the
country out of Salem." Granted, previous repetition of the
antithesis insured closure. But a sequence of antitheses (like
those quoted earlier) may accomplish the same objective if
heard or read for the very first time. That same predictive closure also can evolve from sentences cast in the form leading to
"controls the world" in the sequence quoted earlier.

SUSPENSION AND CLOSURE

People obey another "law" in their customary ways of making sentences: they take the path of least resistance. If some sentence format requires more psychological effort than others to construct, its use likely is avoided. Still another inclination is epitomized by a traditional maxim: "Nearer the heart, nearer the mouth." The more that words signify something important, the more likely they will appear early in a sentence. A sportscaster likely will use this syntax: "He scored a touchdown after breaking through the line, eluding the linebackers, and outrunning the defensive cornerback." The most important words, "He scored a touchdown," occur first in the sentence. The remaining, subordinate or explanatory material then appears after or to the *right* of the kernel subject and predicate. In the common idiom, our sentences usually are "right-branching" this way.

But that sentence can be cast in a "left-branching" conformation: "After breaking through the line, eluding the linebackers, and outrunning the defensive cornerback, he scored a touchdown." In this format, explanatory or qualifying materials appear to the *left* of the kernel subject and predicate. Left-branching sentences are uncommon because important words must be suspended until subordinate material is presented first, and that suspension requires psychological effort. Rather than exert additional energy, communicators more likely start with the subject and predicate and add subordinate materials to the right in what also is called a "loose" or "running" sentence.

Uncommon left-branching sentences are periodic, from the Greek *peri* ("around") and *odos* ("road" or "circular path," whereby someone sees the final destination but must follow a roundabout way to get there, as in the course set for a Greek footrace). Although periodic or left-branching sentences deviate from the common idiom and have some potential for novelty and emphasis, their greater advantage may be derived from redundancy that enhances efficient and accurate closure on the part of respondents. Syntactical placement of subordinate material first in a sentence establishes a semantic context of "information" that facilitates resolution at the end of the statement. Moreover, learning theorists know (as pointed out earlier) that recency has the advantage over primacy, and a periodic suspension puts the important point of the sentence at its end and thereby most recent to the reader or listener.

Left-branching sentences also may project a favorable paramessage of a communicator's caution or judiciousness. In his monumental and widely read history book, *The Influence of Sea Power upon History* (1890), Alfred Thayer Mahan was fond of using periodic sentences as counterpoint to epigrammatic antitheses. Letters to Mahan from naval officers around the world indicated a high regard for the style of his book as it made him appear a cautious, prudent historian whose views should be accepted.[7] Or for application in another rhetorical situation, when graduate students defend their theses or dissertations, opening chapters typically must assert a sentence to the effect that "No one has done any research on this subject except . . . ." But informed readers of such assertions immediately might note in their own minds the exceptions of which they as professors are aware—before the sentences are completed. In a left-branching or periodic format, however, those exceptions are accounted for first: "Except for the studies by Smith at Harvard and Jones at Yale, no one has done any research on this subject." The resultant image is that of prudence and command of one's subject.

HELPFUL HINT *Too many left-branching or periodic sentences in a row can become tiresome, however, particularly when suspensions are long and involved, as in sentences starting with "Although they . . . ," which then add "despite*

*the . . . ," and then insert an "admitting as well of course
the . . . ." By the time the subject and predicate finally occur,
tired respondents have "tuned out." Indeed, even one sentence
with many qualifications standing first may confuse people
who are waiting impatiently for resolution with the suspended
subject and predicate.*

Suspension also accounts for style in "He who controls
Berlin controls Germany; and he who controls Germany controls Europe; and he who controls Europe controls the world."
Yes, this sentence is right-branching, starting with a subject
("He") and predicate ("controls") and then adding words to
the right. Reflecting the axiom about "nearer the heart nearer
the mouth," "controls the world" more likely would come earlier in the sentence, but placement at the end required psychological effort and suspension until subordinate material was
positioned first in a series of steps by degree of importance.
This sentence proceeds from a relatively small unit (a city) to a
larger unit (a country) to the next larger element (a continent)
and finally ends with the largest geographic entity (the world).
Roman rhetoricians called this scheme *scala* (going up a ladder
or "scaling the walls"), *gradatio,* or *incrementum* (the sentence
proceeds by gradual degrees or increments to its conclusion).
The Greeks knew it as *klimax* (a patent progression from the
least significant item through to the most significant). Anticlimax order does not work that way, however, as in "He who
controls the World controls Europe; and he who controls
Europe controls Germany; and he who controls Germany controls _____." Yes, Berlin is a possible completion—but so is
Dresden or Hamburg or Stuttgart or Munich. From the perspective of Information Theory, too many alternatives are available
to attain accurate closure.

In the common idiom, people typically do not exert psychological effort to achieve formal progressions, such as this

one from John Kennedy: "All this will not be finished in the first one hundred days. Nor will it be finished in the first one thousand days, nor in the life of this administration, nor even perhaps in our lifetime on this planet." Each of the successive segments, as depicted below, represents a more significant span of time (with the climax heightened by the *polysyndeton* of *nor* repeated between each one):

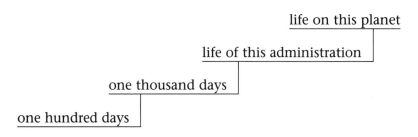

To make a *scala*, *klimax*, or *gradatio*, first visualize a diagram that isolates formal "steps" in a generally understood sequence, such as that from local to state to national, or that from years to decades to centuries, or the following one:

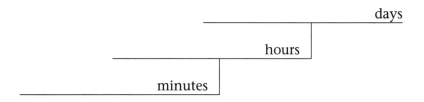

Then, starting in the lowest left-hand blank, write the complete sentence that explains what happened in this hierarchical sequence, such as "The anxiety he first felt for minutes lasted for hours and stayed with him for days."

Some climax suspensions are subtle. The scheme is not always based upon overtly familiar sequences such as that from days to weeks to months to years but rather upon varying semantic nuances. At Gettysburg, Lincoln said, "We cannot dedicate—we cannot consecrate—we cannot hallow this ground" (notice the *anaphora* and *asyndeton*, too). A dedication is comparatively insignificant, with someone snipping a ribbon or turning over the first shovel full of dirt. Consecration, however, requires a religious ceremony that makes the event more momentous. And a hallowed place retains significance for generations to follow. Douglas MacArthur used such climax order at West Point, lauding "duty, honor, country." After all, "duty" entails relatively mundane tasks that someone is required to perform; efforts undertaken for "honor" invariably require greater sacrifice; and endeavors on behalf of "country" may entail soldiers' sacrificing their lives. Similarly, Franklin Roosevelt warned Americans of an impending world war with a series of conditions having subtle shades of importance in meaning for an effect of climax: "To some generations much is given. Of other generations much is expected. This generation of Americans has a rendezvous with destiny" (listeners to a recording of that speech will detect how Roosevelt's vocal variety—of which he was a master—helped heighten the ascending importance of each of the "steps" in the sequence).

If the speaker's intended building blocks of the climax are too subtle in shades of their different meanings to be immediately apparent, an ascending order of importance can be enhanced by inserting appropriate adjectives in front of each item. Suppose a sentence referred to someone's hopes, dreams, and desires. These words are relatively equal in importance. But adjectives can suggest their relative degrees of importance, such as *daily* desires (if they are daily they are comparatively mundane), *fervent* hopes (these are more impressive), and *eternal* dreams (if we have them for an eternity, they must be significant).

A subtle hint of *klimax*, *scala*, or *gradatio* is achieved when key words for the sequence are arranged according to their lengths in alphabet letters or syllables, such as Daniel Webster's reference to "liberty and union, now and forever, one and inseparable." *Union* is pronounced with two syllables; *forever* is said with three; and *inseparable,* with five syllables, is suspended and becomes the largest (most significant?) at the end. Similar rhetorical impress may be attained when lengths of words are not determined by syllables per se but by numbers of letters, as in the U.S. Marine Corps recruiting motto "The few, the proud, the Marines." The hint of climax evolves from progressing from a three letter word, *few,* to the longer *proud,* and ultimately to the longest, *Marines.* The same effect was attained at West Point when General Douglas MacArthur lauded "duty, honor, country," whereby the ascending importance of each word is enhanced by its being progressively longer; the result is increasing impressiveness.

HELPFUL HINT *In some contexts, the opposite of an apparent* scala *or* gradatio *can be the more potent* klimax. *Consider this sentence: "We cannot wait another hour, another minute, another second." Yes, each successive segment is a progressively smaller unit of time, but what seemingly is an anticlimax actually emphasizes urgency—with the same potential for predictive closure. The same holds true in "We must save every quarter, dime, nickel, penny."*

Traditional rhetoricians also recommended a specialized form of *klimax* whereby the last word of a clause is repeated as the first word of the next clause, as in this example from St. Augustine: "We glory in tribulations, knowing that tribulation worketh patience; and patience trial; and trial hope, and hope confoundeth not."[8] Although this variant suggests climax, its seemingly excessive formality displays artificiality that may work to the communicator's disadvantage. Art that calls attention to itself is no longer art. No stylistic device should trumpet its artifice.

In a preceding chapter, communicators were cautioned not to squander repetition upon impotent words unworthy of emphasis. The same principle holds true for schematic climax. Someone might say "He spent a penny, then a nickel, and finally a _____." The amounts are trivial and unworthy of eloquence. But John Kennedy lauded a task that "will not be finished . . . perhaps in our lifetime on this planet." An endeavor that monumental *is* worthy of emphasis derived from style. Efforts on behalf of "I didn't know her for just a few minutes or a couple of hours but several days" or "We are going to have to work at this for seconds, minutes, or even an hour" might lead respondents to conclude that the content was not worth its form—with an ensuing negative reflection upon the communicator. In some other classical advice about style, "The writer who deals with a trivial subject in weighty language is like a man who pretends to qualities he does not possess, undeterred by his lack of them, or like a man who boasts about trifles."[9] So save suspensions for content worthy of emphasis and an audience's psychological participation.

Another observation about climax is pertinent. The word that completes the *scala, klimax*, or *gradatio* should be the last word of a sentence! Do not take an audience up the ladder to an emotional climax—and then add insignificant words to complete the sentence. For example, someone might say, "He strived for months, years, and decades to achieve his position of leadership in the company"; the climax at *decades* is "buried" within the sentence. Greater impress might be attained with "To achieve his position of leadership in the company, he strived for months and years and decades." When the most important word also is emphasized by recency, its significance is heightened. Furthermore, an apt *klimax* or *scala* might elicit applause from an audience (in speechwriters' parlance a "cheer line"). But when speakers proceed "up the ladder" to climaxes that evoke applause and cheering, words occurring thereafter in their sentences are lost.

Despite potential efficacy residing in suspensions, however, parallel repetition may be more powerful. After hearing for the very first time, "of the people, by the people, for the _____," listeners most likely "know" how the statement ends, for a syntactical pattern reduced the amount of information so that closure was virtually assured by the end of the third element. In some situations, speakers might emulate Hubert Humphrey speaking in 1964 as the Democratic candidate for vice-president. His convention acceptance address incorporated successive sentences enumerating values in which Democrats believed—and each one ended alike (*epistrophe* or *antistrophe*) with "But not Senator Goldwater" (the Republican candidate for president). By the third and fourth of his parallel like endings, Humphrey's audience chanted in unison with him, "But not Senator Goldwater." Persuad*ees* articulated the conclusion to be reinforced in their minds by a persuad*er*. Although Walter Mondale tried the same thing in 1980 as the Democratic vice-presidential nominee, a less unified convention prevented his achieving similar closure with the refrain, "But not Ronald Reagan" (Mondale actually told the audience what they were supposed to do vocally). This was not the case, however, for the Democratic vice-presidential candidate in 1992, for Al Gore's parallel like endings of "It's time for them to go" did get the convention audience chanting with him about Republicans. Admittedly, closure as vocal participation might result partly from an audience's "leaning" already in a certain direction attitudinally (as in some religious services wherein preachers' stylistic parallelism helps congregations utter words in unison during a sermon).

Experiments often measure psychological participation with "cloze procedure." Every 10th or 15th word of a text is deleted, and people fill in the blanks. Texts that yield higher scores of accurate completions are more reliable modes of communication (this technique was devised originally to test communicative capabilities of newspapers). And in experimentation comparing effects of passages written in the common idiom with their counterparts rewritten with parallel repetition, style improved closure scores significantly— although message content was not changed.

Rule to Remember

For efficient and accurate closures, like endings are more reliable than like beginnings. Someone could never be certain that *still another* sentence would *begin* with John Kennedy's "Let both sides" or Martin Luther King's "I have a dream." But after "of the people, by the people, for the," prior information from the syntactical pattern itself is sufficient to remove all doubt about how the sequence is destined to end. Like endings are more reliable for closures than like beginnings.

A writing exercise will help you master stylistic redundancy. Compose a speech to persuade that is exactly 100 words long on a current, controversial topic. Then read it aloud to other people deleting exactly every 10th word and clapping your hands instead. When you clap your hands to signify a blank, listeners should be able to write quickly the correct word that goes in each blank. Try to get 100 percent closure scores with redundancy created syntactically by schematic patterns and *not* semantically by *meanings*. You do not want a sequence such as "At Disney World we saw Snow White and the seven _____." Someone filling the blank with *dwarfs* does so because of *semantic* meanings of the previous words (as with *sealed* after "The door was hermetically _____"). You do not want responses determined by what people know or do not know about Disney World (or *hermetically,* for that matter). Attain your goal syntactically so specific prior learning and unique experiences of your respondents likely are not factors. Therefore, this 100-word speech should incorporate *within* its 10-word segments (1) parallel repetitions and (2) antitheses *in sequences* that set up a pattern readily apparent to respondents.

HELPFUL HINT *Do not expect readers or listeners to achieve closure with the second half of your first antithetical pair. Insufficient prior information is available about the pattern. Set up the sequence first, as in "young and old, rich and poor, in war and _____."*

Another format appropriate for this speech is *scala, klimax,* or *gradatio* that yields a readily apparent progression (within 10 words!) to the suspended element of greatest signification. Your objective is to lead respondents, inescapably, to correct closure upon only one alternative about how it ends. Thus, a climax founded formally upon *days, weeks,* and *months* must be followed by a concluding element incorporating *years,* or the pattern might progress from *years* to *decades* to *centuries.*

In writing this exercise, or any discourse, your communicative effectiveness is diminished as you rely primarily on only one scheme to the exclusion of others. Little effort is needed to develop a statement of 100 words wherein 10 sentences of 10 words' length each have the same word for like endings. That speech is monotonous! Any one stylistic technique used too frequently or in too high a concentration becomes boring. Admittedly, in the world of pragmatic affairs, you never will need a statement of exactly 100 words for accurate closure on exactly every 10th word. But if you can "engineer" responses for that degree of exactitude now, you can do virtually anything syntactically later. Mastery will be evident not only in 100 percent accurate scores from respondents but also in their speed of reaction. People should be writing their responses to your 10-word segments at the 8th or 9th word, *before* your handclap signifying the blank. For the pattern is so apparent that accurate closure is achieved with the utmost efficiency for identification between persuader and persuadee.

BROADER IMPLICATIONS OF "FORM"

Redundancy and closure apply as well to organizing the broader dimensions of content in discourse. While preparing public discourse, most speakers already have—or will acquire comparatively easily—substantial amounts of supporting materials for their assertions. With easy availability of materials accumulated by computer access, faxes, published anthologies of quotations, statistical abstracts, and copy machines, speakers no longer have the arduous tasks of finding content for their discourse. The order in which that material is presented, however, raises the issue of organization, or what classical rhetoricians called the canon of *dispositio;* that is, disposing assembled materials into a pattern conducive to persuasion. Although this aspect of discourse is concerned with elements that are larger than sentences, the principles advocated herein about closure are just as applicable. Speeches should progress through some broad pattern whereby their form, like that of stylistic redundancy within sentences, leads to "an arousing and fulfillment of desires . . . insofar as one part of it leads . . . to another part" whereby listeners are "gratified by the experience." Although Information Theory has pertinent applications when arranging words within sentences to capitalize on "the psychology of the *audience*," the same principle may be advantageous when organizing a speech as a whole.

For some rhetorical situations, speakers may structure their persuasive discourse as a "Quest story." Despite its more familiar applications in drama and literature, this "form," identified by Hermann Stelzner as "archetypal," is powerful in the same way as that suggested by the "psychodynamics or orality" described earlier in this book.

> The Quest story is a literary genre in which the subjective experiences of life are central. The themes in such stories vary, but the genre is one of the oldest, hardiest, and most popular. Perhaps its persistent appeal is due to "its validity as a symbolic description of our subjective personal experience of existence as historical." . . . Although the themes and the details change, the form . . . of Quest stories is fairly stable. . . . When the essential elements of the story interact with the subjective experiences of individuals, verbal transactions occur. Occasionally universal human reactions are elicited.

Moreover, in the world of pragmatic affairs, someone typically "speaks and orders a reality, a form; he [or she] offers an *objective* experience of the social, political, or moral life. However, to become viable it must interact with the *subjective* experiences of his [or her] listeners." Five "essential elements" characterize the progression for this potent "rhetorical partition."

> (1) a precious Object and/or Person to be found and possessed or married; (2) a long journey to find the Object, because its whereabouts are not originally known to the seekers; (3) a Hero [or Heroine]; (4) the Guardians of the Object who must be overcome before it can be one; and (5) the Helpers who with their knowledge and/or magical powers assist the Hero [or Heroine] and but for whom he [or she] would never succeed.[10]

The enduring appeal of some motion pictures may stem in part from their plots that are essentially Quest stories, such as that of Dorothy in *The Wizard of Oz* and Scarlett in *Gone With the Wind.*

In many speaking situations, an archetypal Quest form may be appropriate for a wide range of content. It is a typical approach of professional motivational speakers who begin with a "signature story" out of their own experience and proceed to apply the lesson they learned to the life and work of their business audiences. Although Hermann Stelzner illustrated the rhetorical application of this plot line as it was present in President Richard Nixon's speech of November 3, 1969, which outlined his "quest" for peace in Vietnam, the presence of this archetypal form in so many instances of affective communication—whether addresses, drama, literature, or film—suggests its pertinence for a wide range of discourse wherein an ultimate sense of satisfying closure is desired from respondents.

For many rhetorical situations, however, neither the content of a speech nor the speaker's goal lends itself easily for organization as a Quest story. Therefore, a more universally applicable format is appropriate for achieving an ultimate sense of closure on the part of audiences. Recognizing that "most people seek a consistency or *balance* among their cognitions," Alan Monroe and Douglas Ehninger advanced a pattern of speech organization that reflects what John Dewey delineated earlier as "the way in which most individuals, when confronted with a choice or problem situation, systematically think their way through to a decision." As a "dependable psychological basis upon which a speaker can organize a persuasive talk," the "Motivated Sequence" is an effective progression of ideas as the content of a speech:

> Begin by catching the attention of the listeners; direct that attention to a question to be answered or a problem to be solved; next, advance the answer or solution which you believe to be the best; then visualize the advantages to be gained from believing or behaving as you recommend; and, finally, ask the audience for

agreement or action. By adhering to this general progression from question to answer or from problem to
solution, and then on to visualization and action, you
can develop your appeals along the thought line that
most people are accustomed to following.[11]

Having been advocated in editions starting in 1935 by Alan
Monroe, this pattern of organization has proven its applica-
bility for a wide range of discourse over the decades. For in
addition to its providing a format by which speakers' materials can be easily arranged to conform to how audiences
"think their way through to a decision," the motivated
sequence *is* consonant with the desired closure coming from
"Form [that] is an arousing and fulfillment of desires. A work
has form insofar as one part of it leads a reader to another
part, to be gratified by the experience."

BACK TO BASICS

A book about the power of words inevitably must return in
its focus to those nuances of syntax conducing to redundancy
and closure *within* sentences. In the common idiom, syntactical placement of words is highly constrained. After eating a
serving of roast beef and mashed potatoes, a child pushes
away the plate with carrots and peas uneaten—and asks,
"May I have some ice cream for dessert now?" A parent might
say "Don't ask for dessert until you finish your vegetables,"
or, more dogmatically, "Do not ask for dessert until you finish
your vegetables." Such a sentence is not likely to start, "Ask
not for dessert until you . . . ." Nor are English speakers likely
to position an adjective after a noun.

In English, the "actor-action-complement" form of sentence order is the most common. The first position in the
sentence is given to the name of the actor (the subject); the
second position is given to what the actor does (the predi-

cate). Most English sentences reflect this basic actor-action construction. We are free, however, to invert these more common placements, as George Campbell observed about rhetoricians' oft-quoted exemplar from Acts 19:28 and 34:

> No law of the English tongue, relating to the disposition of words in a sentence, holds more generally than this, that the nominative has the first place, the verb the second, and the accusative, if it be an active verb, the participle, adjective, or predicate of whatever denomination it be, occupies the third place. Yet this order, to the great advantage of the expression, is often inverted. Thus, in the general uproar at Ephesus, on occasion of Paul's preaching among them against idolatry, we are informed, that the people exclaimed for some time without intermission, "Great is Diana of the Ephesians."[12]

Freedom to deviate in syntactical placement can lead to several versions of a sentence, such as "The battle of Hastings was fought in 1066" or "In 1066, the battle of Hastings was fought"; but the sentence also can be cast with the inversion, "In 1066, was fought the battle of Hastings."[13] Whenever customary placement of kernel elements is inverted in a sentence, the scheme is called *anastrophe.*

  Some *anastrophes* are subtle. Many people likely would say " . . . who gave their lives here," but Lincoln said, " . . . who here gave their lives." Repositioning *here* not only deviates from the common idiom for word placement but also helps achieve alliteration (for oral discourse) of *who* and *here.* The resultant style, however, evolves from subtle adjustment. Actually, syntactical inversions *should* be subtle. After all, they are intrusions upon our sense of how sentences are cast; for we "know" where certain types of words should be placed. Therefore, kernel elements should not be inverted in ways that prolong the deviation from the common idiom and hold it before the attention of an audience too long. *Anastrophes* using polysyllabic words tend to do this, such as that in "Disadvanta-geous was his position," when the intrusion upon our sensibil-ity is extended over the six syllables in *dis-ad-van-ta-ge-ous.* "Dark was the night" is better.

Rule to Remember

The word to be inverted for an *anastrophe* should be short. A writer or speaker will not want to invert a phrase of sev-eral words, which prolongs the intrusion upon our sense of order.

Repeating the same *anastrophe* as part of like beginnings also is intrusive. Someone might say, "Seek not a higher salary; seek not a more expensive car; seek not a larger house in a more exclusive neighborhood." An audience can tire of the intrusion and react negatively to a sequence that repeats the same inversion at the beginnings of several clauses or sen-tences in sequence.

The best *anastrophe* most likely relies upon uncommon placement of but one, relatively short word. Moreover, that inversion ideally should not extend over a span of more than three or four words. After all, inverting customary word order strains respondents' abilities to handle information comfortably, even to the extent of their not attaining closure with a communicator. Thus, the *Rhetorica Ad Herennium* restricted this scheme to "a transposition confined to two words," and Quintilian similarly indicated that when inver-sion is confined to "two words only, it is called *anastrophe,* that is a reversal of order."[14] In John Kennedy's eminently memorable line, the inversion extends over only two words: "*Ask not* what your country can do for you—ask what you can do for your country" (and thus *three* sources of style were operative on behalf of quotability: AB–BA antithesis, an uncommonly low Type-Token-Ratio, and inversion of two words at the sentence outset).

In Classical, Medieval, and Renaissance treatises on style, rhetoricians often named discrete species of *anastrophe*. If the word was inverted from its more normative position to the start of a sentence, the scheme was *prozeugma* or *prejunctio*; inversion to an ending position was *postjunctio* or *hypozeugma*; and inverting an item from either the end or beginning to the middle of a sentence was *mesezeugma* or *media injunctio*.[15] Rather than dwell on exotic names specifying locations of placement, the more important consideration is the pragmatic function of *anastrophe* to capitalize rhetorically upon laws of primacy and recency (discussed in Chapter 2 about antitheses). Two places in a sentence have a natural advantage for emphasis—the beginning and the end, the word heard first and the one heard last. As Alexander Bain observed, "the least prominent position in the sentence is the MIDDLE. Hence, for giving prominence we must choose either the BEGINNING or the END. . . . The longer the sentence, the more liable are we to flag in the middle portions, while we remember the end, on account of the pause before commencing the next sentence." Adams Sherman Hill also claims that "capital words" deserve to be "at the beginning or the end" of a sentence; and therefore to "fix attention" on the word *murder,* for example, the sentence should read "For Nero's crime against Agrippa the only word is murder."[16] Wherever they occur, however, inversions are discrepant with expectations and create novelty as a factor of attention for resultant emphasis. And if a word is particularly important for a communicator's purposes, normative syntax can be disregarded for an *anastrophe* that leads to a more advantageous placement in the initial or final position.

Inversion that places an important word in the initial position may provide a frame of reference that determines how effectively meaning is communicated as intended. Consider Herbert Spencer's explanation of this familiar *anastrophe*:

> Take the often quoted contrast between "Great is Diana of the Ephesians," and "Diana of the Ephesians is great." When the first arrangement is used, the utterance of the word "great" arouses those vague associations of an impressive nature with which it has been habitually connected; the imagination is prepared to clothe with high attributes whatever follows; and when the words "Diana of the Ephesians" are heard, all the appropriate imagery which can, on the instant, be summarized, is used in the formation of the picture: the mind being thus led directly, and without error, to the intended impression. When, on the contrary, the reverse order is followed, the idea "Diana of the Ephesians" is conceived with no special reference to greatness; and when the words "is great" are added, the conception, has to be remodeled: whence arises a loss of mental energy, and a corresponding diminution of effect.[17]

An important goal of effective public speakers or any communicators, then, is to establish a context in which their topics are viewed for greater advantage; and in those instances, inversion of a capital word to the initial sentence position is appropriate.

Inversion placing an important word last in a sentence, however, may be suitable because of emphasis derived from recency, particularly as it is enhanced by the customary moment of silence following the last word of a sentence or the additional space on the printed page following the period. An attorney named Joseph Welch was retained as legal counsel by the U.S. Army to counter charges made by Senator Joseph McCarthy during the Army-McCarthy Hearings in the 1950s (a Senate committee was investigating McCarthy's charges during the Cold War that the U.S. Army coddled

Communists in its ranks). At one pivotal point, after an unwarranted statement by McCarthy, Welch asked, "Have you no sense of decency, sir? At long last? Have you left no sense of decency?" *Decency* was the word worthy of emphasis, but it would have been obscured in its more normative placement, "Have you no sense of decency left?" The inverted syntax for *left* places the important word, *decency,* in a more advantageous position (and the span of words over which the *anastrophe* extends is only four, short words). And as indicated in the earlier chapter about antitheses, the same axiom held true for even the most subtle of a speaker's subtle adjustments: "a main difference . . . between orator and orator really does lie in the aptness with which they arrange their words."

NOTES

1. I review this empirical research in my essay, "Stylistic Redundancy and Function in Discourse," *Language and Style* 3 (Winter 1970): 62–68.

2. Floyd Allport, *Theories of Perception and the Concept of Structure* (New York: John Wiley and Sons, 1955): 213 and Donald E. Broadbent, *Perception and Communication* (London, 1958): 118.

3. T. Karwoski and J. Schacter, "Psychological Studies in Semantics: III. Reaction Time for Similarity and Difference," *Journal of Social Psychology* 38 (1948): 103–120. See also my discussion in Chapter 2."

4. Kenneth Burke, "Psychology and Form" and "Lexicon Rhetoricae," both in *Counter-Statement* (Lost Altos, CA: Hermes Publications, 1931): 30–31, 124, 138.

5. Kenneth Burke, *A Rhetoric of Motives* (New York, 1958): 21, 49–51, 55–69.

6. Longinus *On the Sublime* 7, translated by H. L. Havell (London, 1890). Other rhetoricians attest to the same capability of style. See George Campbell, *The Philosophy of Rhetoric* (1776), ed. Lloyd Bitzer (Carbondale, IL: University of Southern Illinois Press, 1963): 121 as well as Hugh Blair, *Lectures on Rhetoric and Belles Lettres* (London, 1787), Vol. II, Lecture Nineteen, p. 35.

7. See, for instance, Ronald H. Carpenter, "Alfred Thayer Mahan's Style on Sea Power: A Paramessage Conducing to *Ethos,*" *Speech Monographs* 42 (August 1975): 190–202 or Chapter 4 in Carpenter, *History as*

Rhetoric: Style, Narrative, and Persuasion (Columbia, SC: University of South Carolina Press, 1995).

8. St. Augustine *De Doctrina Christiana Liber Quartus* 7. 11, translated by Sister Therese Sullivan (Washington, D.C.: Catholic University Press, 1930).

9. Demetrius *On Style* 119.

10. Hermann G. Stelzner, "The Quest Story and Nixon's November 3, 1969 Address," *Quarterly Journal of Speech* 57 (April 1971): 163–164. Stelzner's quotation incorporated in his opening paragraph is from W. H. Auden, "The Quest Hero," *Texas Quarterly* 4 (Winter 1961): 82.

11. See Alan H. Monroe and Douglas Ehninger, *Principles of Speech Communication*, Sixth Brief Edition (Glenview, IL: Scott, Foresman and Company, 1969): 259–261.

12. Campbell, 355. This particular quotation is a favorite of rhetoricians who explicate eloquent style in discourse. See, for instance, Richard Whately, *Elements of Rhetoric* (1828), ed. Douglas Ehninger (Carbondale: Southern Illinois University Press, 1963): 313; and Henry Day, *The Art of Discourse*, 7th ed. (New York: Scribner, Armstrong, and Company, 1875): 327–328.

13. Alexander Bain, *English Composition and Rhetoric*, Enlarged Ed., (London: Longmans, Green and Company, 1890): 11.

14. *Rhet. Ad Her.* iv. 32. 44. and Quintilian *Institutes of Oratory* viii. 6, 65, translated by H. E. Butler (London: William Heinemann Ltd., 1960). Because he also perceived *anastrophe* as limited to a transposition of two words, Richard Sherry called the scheme *"reversio."* See his *Treatise of Schemes and Tropes* (1550), in a facsimile reproduction with introduction by Herbert W. Hildebrandt (Gainesville: Scholars' Facsimiles and Reprints, 1961): A2r-v.

15. I compiled the various names of these syntactical devices in "The Essential Schemes of Syntax: An Analysis of Rhetorical Theory's Recommendations for Uncommon Word Orders," *Quarterly Journal of Speech* 55 (April 1969): 161–168.

16. Adams Sherman Hill, *The Principles of Rhetoric* (New York: American Book Company, 1895): 184–185.

17. Herbert Spencer, "The Philosophy of Style," in *The Art of the Writer*, ed. Lane Cooper (Ithaca: Cornell University Press, 1952): 245–246.

A ppendix

ABOUT DELIVERY

Delivery, I assert, is the dominant factor in oratory; without delivery the best speaker cannot be of any account at all.

Cicero, *De Oratore*

The potential persuasiveness of orality is likely achieved only to the extent that speakers' vocal and physical mannerisms complement the form and content of their statements. Even the best words in their best orders are impotent if their delivery is deficient. As the consummate orator, Cicero emphasized the role of effective delivery as it contributed to persuasiveness:

> But the effect of all of these oratorical devices depends on how they are delivered. Delivery, I assert, is the dominant factor in oratory; without delivery the best speaker cannot be of any account at all, and a moderate speaker with a trained delivery can often outdo the best of them. The story goes that when Demosthenes was asked what is the first thing in speaking, he assigned the first role to delivery, and also the second, and also the third.[1]

In the age of the all-seeing and omnipresent television camera, Americans *know* what constitutes effective delivery of oral discourse. And they recognize the difference between speakers whose delivery is deficient and those who are adept (such as the marked dichotomy during the presidential debates in 1980 between an oratorically inept Jimmy Carter and an articulate Ronald Reagan). So several guidelines, likely known already to many speakers, nevertheless merit brief reiteration here.

VOCAL VARIETY

Speakers consciously can control three of the four vocal variables: (1) rate of speaking in words per minute, (2) force or loudness of the voice, and (3) pitch variation. The fourth vocal variable, quality (such as nasality or hoarseness), is less easily controlled during delivery of speeches. Of the three variables easily within speakers' control, rate is particularly important. For native speakers of English, normative conversational rate can be approximately 140 to 150 words per minute (approximately 2 words per second). So this rate is one that listeners are accustomed to, perceptually and cognitively. Speaking that exceeds a normative rate, particularly for long durations of time, poses a problem: because people tend to follow the path of least resistance, listeners who must exert too much energy to keep up with a speaker's rapidity often tune out. Conversely, if someone speaks too slowly, an audience also may tune out because of boredom. Yes, some statements demand slower speaking to enhance their impress. General Douglas MacArthur, for example, was adept at sensing when slow delivery was appropriate. In his famous speech to a Joint Meeting of Congress in 1951, the final paragraph of 128 words, which included "old soldiers never die; they just fade away," took 94 seconds to deliver (an average of 1.36 words per second). In his famous address at West Point about "Duty, honor, country," the General's last 55 words, in a barely audible voice, required 56 seconds to deliver! But virtually one word per second was appropriate when saying with emotion, "my last conscious thoughts will be of the corps, and the corps, and the corps."[2]

Pitch, or the relative highness or lowness of the speaker's voice, requires only one pertinent statement of advice: avoid monotone! Speaking continuously at the same level of pitch soon will have an audience bored (if not asleep). Listen to yourself speaking on an audio- or videotape recording. If your pitch is unchanging, strive to inject more variation in your sentences (but not that of a "mechanical, sing-song" nature). Television newscasters invariably have well-modulated voices that demonstrate favorable flexibility in pitch levels while speaking. Because their voices are heard for a substantial number of minutes of continuous talking during telecasts, maintaining audience attention is facilitated by avoiding monotones. Listen to their varied pitch levels and emulate that delivery. After all, one of the most natural of human endeavors in many communication situations is to imitate vocal mannerisms of those people from whom we want acceptance, for one of the most reliable means of securing that acceptance is to talk the way those people talk.

Effective speakers also vary the levels of force or loudness with which their words are uttered. The guideline for force is simple: some words in sentences are more important than others, so say them louder. Many speakers underline important words in the text from which they deliver their statements; those cues remind speakers to say those words louder. In the final analysis, appropriate vocal variety is relatively easy to attain in public speaking. After all, in ordinary day-to-day conversation, vocal variety typically is natural. In an adage expressed in many public speaking textbooks, effectiveness is enhanced, in many communication situations, when the endeavor is approached as one of "conversing with an audience."

MOVEMENT AND GESTURE

Gesture refers to parts of the body, particularly arms and hands, helping the speaker communicate; movement refers to the entire body changing position by stepping backward or forward, for instance, or purposefully stepping to one side or another, most likely to help suggest transitions from one topic in the speech to another. In our natural communication endeavors, we are physically animated, using gestures as well as physical movement and various aspects of "body language" to help communicate our ideas. For many professional presentations, however, lecterns and microphones will inhibit speakers' physical movement, particularly when they are offering their statements to large audiences from complete and carefully crafted word-for-word manuscripts. Those speakers are unlikely to move from the lectern and its microphone (or TelePrompTer).

Nevertheless, even when constrained by lecterns, speakers' arms and hands still are free for purposeful gesture to point, enumerate, or indicate acceptance or rejection, for instance. So avoid getting a "death grip" on the sides of a lectern, as many inexperienced speakers do, for that tenacious hold inhibits the use of hands to help communicate ideas. In summational effect, when complemented by speakers' vocal variety, delivery from behind a lectern can be as favorably animated as that in lively conversation.

When giving extemporaneous speeches, that is, from a carefully developed outline, and when not confined to lecterns and their microphones, speakers can step from side to side or backward and forward to suggest transitions or emphases. Even for larger audiences, portable microphones can be attached to the speaker's clothing to allow that flexibility of purposeful movement to help communicate information. The fact of the matter is that movement, whether of the body or a part of the body, attracts the eye, and attention focused on the speaker is thus facilitated. This commentary, however, is not an endorsement of random movement or any physical activity that does not help the speaker communicate, such as pacing back and forth across the platform or folding or rolling and unrolling sheets of paper that contain the speaker's outline or text. For the most effective public speaking, gestures and movements must be purposeful.

DIRECTNESS

Directness does not mean simply looking in the direction of an audience! Speakers can face physically in the direction of their audiences but still be psychologically oblivious to how those listeners are reacting. Directness is the singularly important attribute whereby effective communicators are constantly aware of how their listeners are reacting. For only by attending to audience responses can speakers know, for instance, the extent to which listeners need further explanation or whether they can hear easily. Maintaining directness is difficult, of course, when delivering a speech from a word-for-word manuscript that must be read aloud, and in these situations, speakers must be sufficiently familiar with their material that they can glance down, take in a phrase or two in an instant, and look right back up at their audiences. After all, only with directness can speakers truly engage their audiences psychologically by looking them in the eyes (as done during effective conversations with people). Perhaps no other facet of delivery demonstrates speakers' genuine interest in their audiences more than does directness.

As an illustration, when I was an undergraduate, I had won at my college the privilege to be a speaker in a prestigious intercollegiate oratorical contest at another university. My carefully crafted, word-for-word text for the oration was memorized as required for that speaking event. Given an afternoon opportunity to rehearse in the auditorium in which the contest would be held that evening, I stood on the stage and practiced reciting my speech from memory. The professor who accompanied me as my oratory coach immediately sensed that my attention as a speaker was focused inwardly on remembering the words I would utter. So he walked around the empty auditorium and interrupted me every few sentences, saying, "What was that you just said?" or, "I didn't hear that last word." Becoming exasperated, I in turn began following his every move with my eyes, speaking directly to him to make sure that he heard every word exactly as I intended. In that short time, he conditioned me to focus my attention outwardly upon him as a listener rather than inwardly upon the "TelePrompTer" of my memory. That new sense of directness carried over to that evening as I spoke to several hundred people attending the event. Although audiences that large heretofore tended to be a blur to me, as I experienced some stagefright, every face that night was crystal clear. Perhaps I looked so carefully at my audience in part to find my oratory coach (I eventually spotted him sitting in the last row of seats—and noticed his cupping his hand behind his ear to indicate that I should speak louder), but the overall directness that I achieved undoubtedly contributed to my success that night as a speaker.

The same directness is the *sine qua non* undergirding the effectiveness of all oral presentations. A prize-winning author and observer of political personae recently had a pertinent observation about the importance of directness. Epitomizing President Bill Clinton's capabilities as a speaker, Bob Woodward said, "He's the communicator of all time . . . [President] Reagan was good, but not even in the ballpark with Clinton." Recalling a conversation with Clinton in the Oval Office, Woodward said, "The man was drilling me with eye contact." And whereas "most of us waste our eyes," Clinton's directness contributed to an effect whereby listeners believe "he can really understand you. . . . You have the feeling that somehow there is total agreement."[3] So to conclude, my final directive is on behalf of directness: eloquence that works works best when enhanced by eye contact.

NOTES

1. Cicero *De Oratore* III. 213. See the translation by Horace Rackham in the Loeb Classical Library (Cambridge, MA: Harvard University Press, 1948).

2. For detailed discussion of the General's public speaking and its effects, see Bernard K. Duffy and Ronald H. Carpenter, *Douglas MacArthur, Warrior as Wordsmith* (New York: Greenwood, 1997).

3. Robert Woodward's speech at the University of Florida was quoted at length in the *Gainesville Sun*, April 16, 1998.

About Toastmasters International

If the thought of public speaking is enough to stop you dead in your tracks, it may have the same effect on your career.

While surveys report that public speaking is one of people's most dreaded fears, the fact remains that the inability to effectively deliver a clear thought in front of others can spell doom for professional progress. The person with strong communication skills has a clear advantage over tongue-tied colleagues—especially in a competitive job market.

Toastmasters International, a nonprofit educational organization, helps people conquer their pre-speech jitters. From one club started in Santa Ana, California, in 1924, the organization now has more than 170,000 members in 8,300 clubs in 62 countries.

How Does It Work?

A Toastmasters club is a "learn by doing" workshop in which men and women hone their communication and leadership skills in a friendly, supportive atmosphere. A typical club has 20 members who meet weekly or biweekly to practice public speaking techniques. Members, who pay approximately $35 in dues twice a year, learn by progressing through a series of 10 speaking assignments and being evaluated on their performance by their fellow club members. When finished with the basic speech manual, members can select from among 14 advanced programs that are geared toward specific career needs. Members also have the opportunity to develop and practice leadership skills by working in the High Performance Leadership Program.

Besides taking turns to deliver prepared speeches and evaluate those of other members, Toastmasters give impromptu talks on assigned topics, usually related to current events. They also develop listening skills, conduct meetings, learn parliamentary procedure and gain leadership experience by serving as club officers. But most importantly, they develop self-confidence from accomplishing what many once thought impossible.

The benefits of Toastmasters' proven and simple learning formula has not been lost on the thousands of corporations that sponsor in-house Toastmasters clubs as cost-efficient means of satisfying their employees' needs for communication training. Toastmasters clubs can be found in the U.S. Senate and the House of Representatives, as well as in a variety of community organizations, prisons, universities, hospitals, military bases, and churches.

How to Get Started

Most cities in North America have several Toastmasters clubs that meet at different times and locations during the week. If you are interested in forming or joining a club, call (714) 858-8255. For a listing of local clubs, call (800) WE-SPEAK, or write Toastmasters International, PO Box 9052, Mission Viejo, California 92690, USA. You can also visit our website at http://www.toastmasters.org.

As the leading organization devoted to teaching public speaking skills, we are devoted to helping you become more effective in your career and daily life.

Terrence J. McCann
Executive Director, Toastmasters International

Allyn & Bacon presents...
The Essence of Public Speaking series

Endorsed by Toastmasters International

"These excellent books are ideal for [those] who want to offer practical ideas about the wonderful world of paid speaking... and are also ideal for those who want to speak to promote their professions, careers, or causes. The *Essence of Public Speaking* books are easy to understand, and simple to activate."

— Dottie Walters, President, Walters International Speakers Bureau,
Publisher, Sharing Ideas Magazine for Speakers, and Author of Speak & Grow Rich

Choosing Powerful Words: Eloquence That Works, by Ronald Carpenter

"If you are serious about speaking, this book will be an invaluable aid."

Dilp R. Abayasekara, Ph.D., DTM, CEO Speakers Services Unlimited,
Toastmasters International Accredited Speaker

Delivering Dynamic Presentations: Using Your Voice and Body for Impact, by Ralph Hillman

"This is not only a MUST READ, it is a MUST LIVE book."

Jan M. Roelofs, Communications Consultant

Involving Your Audience: Making It Active, by Karen Lawson

"This book is chock full of tips and techniques that can help turn any presentation into an interactive gold mine."

George Morrisey, CSP, CPAE, author of *Morrisey on Planning*

Speaking for Impact: Connecting with Every Audience, by Shirley Nice

" This is a MUST READ for any speaker that wants to speak from the inside out."

Terry Paulson, Ph.D., professional speaker on *Making Change Work* and 1998-1999
President, National Speakers Association

Motivating Your Audience: Speaking from the Heart, by Hanoch McCarty

"This book reflects Hanoch McCarty's many years of experience and his incredibly inventive mind."

Jack Canfield, co-author of *Chicken Soup for the Soul*

See Inside Front Cover for a Complete Listing
of the Essence of Public Speaking Books